RISE OF AN AMERICAN GANGSTRESS

PART 2

Buy

for Melodrama

RISE OF AN AMERICAN GANGSTRESS
PART 2

KIM K.

Rise of an American Gangstress Part 2. Copyright © 2013 by Melodrama Publishing. All rights reserved. Printed in the United States of America. No part of this book may be used or reproduced in any manner whatsoever without written permission except in the case of brief quotations embodied in critical articles or reviews. For information, address Melodrama Publishing, P.O. Box 522, Bellport, NY 11713.

www.melodramapublishing.com

Library of Congress Control Number: 2013946108
ISBN-13: 978-1620780220
First Edition: October 2013
10 9 8 7 6 5 4 3 2 1

Interior Design: Candace K. Cottrell
Cover Design: Marion Designs
Model: Kamale

ALSO BY KIM K.

PROLOGUE

Somewhere outside of Medellín, Colombia,
September 11, 2012

The M2 Browning firearm was an intimidating piece of hardware. The .50 caliber machine gun was meant for one purpose only: to brutally kill everything in its path. The eyes that looked down the barrel of the large, lethal weapon radiated with terror and trepidation. The kidnapped family was huddled tightly together in fear, as if they had an invisible shield around them to prevent any harm headed their way. But there was no shield of protection, only the inevitable   death.

The crew scowling at them was dressed in fatigues and was heavily armed with automatic shotguns and assault rifles. They resembled the men in the American forces, but this wasn't a guerilla or paramilitary group at war with an unjust government. These men were hardcore killers—assassins, with hundreds of violent murders stained into their souls, desensitized to any type of life or humanity. This was the setting of an assassination of a family of four. Lined up near the thick brush of trees, were Marisol, her husband Santana, their six-year-old daughter, Nelda and their ten-year-old son, Hector.

There wasn't any need for duct tape or restraints, or loud music to cover their screams. No one would hear their cries or the calls for help.

Everyone was miles away from civilians or villages. The thick, tall trees, the wild grass, and the rough shrubberies went on for miles on the rolling hills that seemed never-ending. The nearest road to any type of town was twenty-five miles away. It was a desolate area. They were in the heart of the jungle.

All four casualties of the drug war stood defiant, including ten-year-old Hector. He was small, only a boy, but remained stoic. The half-dozen men and one woman that surrounded the family with their artillery were all stone-faced. They had two missions: Find the location of Pablo, and kill all four victims.

"Tell us where your grandpa hides Pablo and we will promise to make the killings clean and quick," the woman said in Spanish.

Her attention was directed at little Hector. Marisol, Santana and Nelda were of no value to her. She towered over the little boy with the assault rifle gripped in her hand; her expression toward him was cold like an Alaskan winter. She wanted information. The parents, Marisol and Santana, were born under the code of the drug cartel, and they wouldn't dare give up such priceless information under any circumstance. They had taken an oath when they began running their syndicate, and Marisol's bloodline wouldn't allow her to betray her father.

It was a silent rule that the firstborn would be fed all pertinent family secrets from the age of seven. This was important in their culture because it was likely the father would be assassinated. And if the head of the household was taken out, his son would be able to follow in his footsteps and sustain the family. In this case, Santana wasn't the head of the household, it was Marisol. Her father was Jesus, and he was the wealthiest and most feared man in South America's history.

Jesus' organization brought in ten billion dollars in drug money annually. Jesus sat in meetings with presidents of third-world countries and was treated as an ambassador of Colombia. He spent millions a year on weapons and paid off officials in five countries to have diplomatic immunity. He had over a dozen legitimate foundations that gave money to cancer research and the AIDS epidemic. But none of that would help his daughter, Marisol, and her family at the moment. Their kidnappers didn't care about her father's pedigree, they only wanted information and to see bloodshed. At that very moment, Marisol was on her way to hell, and her family—the immediate and even distant—would be joining her soon.

Little Hector glared at the woman standing over him and shouted in Spanish, "I tell you nothing!"

He was defiant. It was something unexpected from him. The only hope of finding Pablo would be if Hector told them the location. The young boy was fuming and had his hands balled into fists. He glared at the clan of assassins with unadulterated hatred for them. He was too young to fully understand death, and he wasn't going to disappoint his parents. Hector had been telling his father for over a year now that he was a man. And in his mind, it was time to prove it.

Hector's rebelliousness would become costly, though. The ringleader, the dark woman—petite in black fatigues with her long, black hair styled into a bushy ponytail, standing five-seven, her eyes cold and threatening—nodded her head once to her lieutenant. He didn't hesitate to execute her silent order. He stepped toward Santana with the pistol in his hand, raised it to the man's head and fired without any wavering at all. Santana dropped to the ground like a heavy sack of potatoes. The only person who outwardly showed any emotion was Nelda. She burst into tears and ran to her father.

"Papa…! Papa…! Mi Papa…!" she cried out as she fell to her knees, clutching her papa's dead body and kissed his bloody face. She continued to cry out as Marisol and Hector didn't flinch.

The cold woman turned to look at Marisol and Hector. Through clenched teeth, she said in Spanish, "That was to prove we could have mercy and kill without torture. I am going to ask you one more time for the location of Pablo. If you do not tell me, then we will hacksaw and carve your sister into tiny pieces. We will see how strong you and your mama are."

Marisol tried to maintain her strength and equanimity, but the threat of having her young daughter ripped apart brutally was terrifying. She remained silent; a single tear fell from her eye. The woman nodded to her lieutenant, and he walked toward Nelda with a machete in his hand as the little girl continued to cry over her father.

"Wait!" Marisol spoke up. "As a mother…"

Hector interjected, "Mama, don't tell them!"

"Silencio!" Marisol screamed out.

It was the first time she had shown any emotion since she and her family were kidnapped. Marisol continued with, "As a mother, if I can spare one child then I am half decent. You already know we will not tell you the location of Pablo. But if you promise that you will not harm Nelda, I will tell you where my fortune is hidden. Take Nelda back to our village and she will be taken care of. She is harmless. She is a little girl and will not seek revenge when she comes of age. She is different than Hector. She is different than you or I. Please . . . have mercy on my child."

The woman in fatigues stepped toward Marisol with a steely stare. She stood inches from her and proclaimed through her gritted teeth, "I was taught that when you go to your enemy and ask for help, never plead for mercy, because your enemy won't have any for you. You should have made a petition toward my interest, which is Pablo, and Nelda would have been spared. You should have given up a life for a life. Pablo's life would have saved Nelda's life. Now I will torture you, and while you're in hell you will be tormented, not knowing how your children were murdered!"

More tears fell from Marisol's eyes. The only thing she felt she could barter with was money and, she realized quickly, they only had one goal, and that was Pablo. There wasn't any way Marisol could give him up. Why put Pablo's life in danger when it wouldn't spare theirs? And even if she did give up Pablo and Nelda's life was spared, it wouldn't be for long. Nelda would be murdered by Jesus for the family's betrayal.

"Who are you?" Marisol wanted to know.

"La Dama de la Mafia," the cold woman replied.

"You lie!" Marisol spat on the ground to show her disgust. "She is dead! My father killed her!"

If they were to die, then they would die as a family. She accepted her fate. Quickly, three men pounced on her and forcefully threw her to the ground in front of her children. Hector stood still with a brave stare. He breathed heavily and tried to hold back his tears. He wanted to believe that he was a man, but the boy in him was surely emerging as tears leaked from his eyes. He couldn't save his mother from her fate.

They restrained Marisol to the ground. She tried to fight them off, but their strength was overwhelming. They extended her right arm; there was a knee pressed against her neck and her other arms held down. The weight of the second man was pressed against her chest, and the third revealed a hacksaw in his hand. Marisol's eyes widened with fear; she squirmed, but not much. It felt like gravity was against her.

The dark woman in fatigues went over to Hector and grabbed the back of his neck tightly. It was a crushing grip against his young flesh. He cringed. She held him steady and instructed him to watch.

"This is your mother's fate," she said chillingly.

He could only watch as they used the hacksaw to cut into his mother's flesh, her arm ripped apart by the tool. Her screams were loud and terrifying. Sheer pain engulfed her, and she screamed and screamed as the rusty blade cut through her thin arm little by little. There was blood everywhere, and the cries echoed throughout the jungle. When they were done with her right arm, they hacked away at her left, then her legs. The process was a lengthy one, and soon, there was no more screaming. They had butchered her. Nelda was hysterical. Hector's eyes were flooded with tears. Marisol's last words to her butchers were pleas for them to not subject her children to the same type of torture. Marisol stayed alive until she couldn't live anymore.

With his mother hacked apart, he was asked one last time for the location of Pablo. He remained defiant. The damage had already been done. He spit in the face of his captor and grimaced.

"Puta!" he shouted.

His rebellious nature had been ingrained since his birth. He was solid as a rock and wouldn't break or fold. The heat of the jungle began to get taxing. Once again, the leader gave a head nod and a bullet was put into Hector's young skull. The catatonic Nelda sat quietly against a tree with her thumb lodged into her mouth. Her father and mother's murder had broken the little girl.

"What about Nelda?" one of the men asked.

The woman, like she was giving an order to kill a pig, effortlessly said, "Kill her!"

CHAPTER 1

Fancy rested the back of her head against the headrest of the moving SUV and sighed heavily. She closed her eyes and thought about how far she had come since her mother's arrest. She had gone from being a naive teenager to almost running her own empire and having endless respect on the streets. She wasn't clueless anymore, and since the murders, she felt her heart transforming into a pillar of ice. There was only one way to go, and that was up. The bottom was not a place for her.

Nasir was driving, doing 55 mph on the highway with the radio playing Rick Ross and pulling on a cigarette. He was quiet during the ride to MDC, the federal prison in Brooklyn, New York. He didn't have much to say to Fancy, and Fancy didn't have much to say to him. Nasir had noticed the change in Fancy, and he started to feel somewhat dubious about their relationship. It seemed like the changing of the guard on the streets, with him becoming the Robin and Fancy becoming the Batman. The starters in the game were now seated on the bench, and the second string players were in the game and maybe on their way to winning a championship.

The traffic was light in the borough, and the sky was as blue as a Smurf. It was a beautiful morning with a little winter briskness. Fancy felt a little apprehensive about meeting with her mother. Belen was the real queen-pin who'd had her father murdered, and the secrets were starting to spill. But her mother had summoned her, and she didn't want to tell her no. Belen was a dangerous woman who Fancy didn't want to cross. Even incarcerated, Belen had showed that she still had reach. And since the truth was revealed about her past, it gave Fancy certain clarity about her future.

Nasir pulled in front of the towering brick and ironclad, grayish-looking building with barbed wire and bars on the windows. It was a hideous fortress that housed some of the most dangerous inmates. It was federal lockup and most likely would be her mother's permanent home, until death did her apart. It was a place Fancy couldn't imagine spending the rest of her life inside.

Fancy stepped out of the gleaming black SUV, clad in a gray, quarter-length mink coat and a black Fendi dress and her Jimmy Choo stilettos. She had special plans after visiting her mother. Her life still went on while Belen's was at a permanent standstill.

Nasir decided to wait in the vehicle. He wasn't too thrilled to visit his aunt Belen. This was Fancy's business, not his. He sparked up another Newport, took a few deep pulls, exhaled, and turned up the radio and watched as Fancy strutted toward the front entrance of the federal fortress. It gave him chills just being outside the prison. While Fancy was inside, he would get on his phone and make a few important phone calls of his own. Business never stopped, no matter where he was.

Fancy disappeared into the building. It was swarming with correction officers and other authorities in dark uniforms. And for a prison, the place was immaculate, the floors buffed and polished, and everything orderly. Fancy knew the routine: Empty everything out of your pockets, move through the metal detectors slowly, state who you were there to see, their relation to you, and the reason for the visit. She had to sign her name and be patient. She was in their house now, and the rules were strict. Some of the guards at the front entrance already knew who Fancy was. They smiled at her but still executed their job to the fullest.

Fancy fixed her eyes on the female inmates that started piling into the room, their eyes quickly searching for their loved ones spread throughout the visiting room. More smiles than frowns showed.

Belen was the last one to enter the room. She looked around with a deadpan expression. It seemed to Fancy that her mother was always angry. Her black hair was styled into long cornrows, making her look somewhat like a dyke, a look Fancy was getting used to. Her eyes were cold and sunken in, and the bleak brown attire she wore clung loosely to her thin frame.

Belen had seen better days, but as each day inside MDC went by, she was losing her classiness and zeal. The system was tearing her down little by little, but she refused to admit it. She eyed her daughter who sat some distance toward the back and felt some minor hatred for her her daughter was looking fine, her shapely figure clad in a stylish dress, her long, sensuous black hair looking marvelous. Seeing Fancy looking so refined reminded Belen of the good old days when she was young and extremely beautiful, with all the men chasing her.

The two women locked eyes, and Belen seated herself immediately. There weren't any long, loving hugs, kisses, or genuine hellos. Belen just wanted to get down to business with her daughter. Her face was rigid. They didn't have time for useless chitchat.

"Hey Mommy," Fancy greeted dryly.

"You look nice," she replied halfheartedly.

"Thanks . . ."

Fancy shifted in her seat and re-crossed her legs. She continued to look at her mother. The layers had been peeled back from her moms and Fancy was able to see the true Belen. She didn't smile as much and her eyes showed callousness.

"I'm being transferred to a different prison in less than eight months. The feds are sending me to Hazelton," Belen said roughly.

Fancy didn't even know where Hazelton was. It was like getting hit with a brick.

"Hazelton, where the heck is that?" she asked, displeased by the news.

"West Virginia," Belen replied nonchalantly.

"West Virginia! Are they fuckin' crazy?" Fancy shouted in shock, drawing some minor attention to herself from others seated in the room.

The female correction officer by the door shot Fancy a stern look, giving her a warning about her outburst. Fancy scowled at the overweight bitch, being far from intimidated by anyone anymore.

Fancy couldn't see her mother being transferred so far away. How far was West Virginia? And wasn't it a redneck state? It was bad enough she was locked down in a federal prison, but now they were trying to remove Belen from her life completely.

"This shit probably wouldn't be happening if I had a decent lawyer to represent me," Belen chided. Belen twisted her face with contempt and added, "That damn lawyer you hired wasn't shit. Incompetent muthafucka!"

"I did my best under the conditions and circumstances surrounding us, Mommy," Fancy argued.

"If that was your best, then I would hate to see your worst," she quipped back. "If you hadn't allowed the Feds to get their hands on our money, then I would have had very good representation and probably wouldn't be doing life in prison. You gonna need to come up with another half a million to retain the services of Gary Scheck, Fancy. The person you should have hired to represent me in the first fucking place."

Fancy frowned at her mother, thinking she was an ungrateful fucking bitch. It wasn't her fault her mother had lied about everything from the time of her birth, and burned every bridge with her sister, Brenda. Fancy was her only support, and Belen needed to recognize and start being a little more respectful.

Fancy also didn't want to continue speaking about her past. She was no longer that naive girl. She had gone through too much in a short time. She had lost the man she'd thought was her real father, Alexandro, and found out that her parents weren't upstanding citizens but international drug distributors. Friends were turning into enemies, and she was a cold-blooded murderer. As Biggie once said, "Things done changed."

Fancy wanted to change the subject. She wanted information from her mother. She wanted to know more about her connect. She wanted to know about Jesus. Just because her mother was fucked up didn't mean she had to be.

Fancy locked eyes with Belen. She erected herself in her seat, adjusted the length in her dress, and leaned in closer to her mother. She didn't have time to beat around the bush. Belen wanted something from her, and she needed something from Belen.

"I need to get with your connect, Mommy. I need to speak to Jesus. Can you get me a meeting with him? I know it's my time," Fancy said with some authority in her tone.

Belen cut her eyes at Fancy, and the hard frown on her face showed her reluctance. Jesus was a dangerous man, and Belen feared the repercussions if Fancy didn't follow the rules. She knew Fancy wasn't ready yet, even with Nasir by her side. This was a completely different ball game—from the minors to the majors in a heartbeat—and not everybody was cut out to play in the major league.

"I'm ready to meet him, my father. I wanna know what he's like and get into business with him," she said with conviction.

Belen remained quiet for a moment. She averted her eyes from Fancy and cast them down at the floor. She was in heavy thought about something.

"I need to meet my real father. I'm tired of the lies and deceit in my life since the day I was born. It's time for me to confront everything you tried to hide from me," she added in a stern tone.

Unbeknownst to Fancy, Belen didn't have a choice. Belen had summoned Fancy not only for her self-interest, but because it was a direct order from Jesus. He finally wanted a meeting with Fancy. Belen was concerned, but Jesus was not to be denied what he wanted.

Belen focused her attention back on her daughter. "He wants to meet with you too."

Fancy was elated. She wanted to do a backflip from her seat and do cartwheels around the room. It was the best news she'd heard in a long time. She smiled and wanted to leap across the table and hug her mother. But she kept her composure. Fancy secretly hoped that her father would embrace her and treat her like Alexandro once treated her, his young princess, even though their relationship had been a lie.

Jesus was the largest drug trafficker in international history since Pablo Escobar. Jesus was a true descendant of Escobar and just as ruthless—or more so. People said that instead of blood, cyanide ran through his veins. His name begot legends, and some said that his skin was cold to touch and he was the walking dead. He didn't have any emotions. He was always stoic. Some said he was murdered years ago and his ghost still haunted the family members of his victims. And there were some who said he was in the federal witness protection program and living in Utah, hiding in a Mormon village. Jesus was many things in everyone's eyes, but the most accurate depiction of him was that he was truly feared and powerful.

Fancy couldn't wait to meet her biological father. There were so many questions she wanted to ask him, so many things she wanted to know and learn. She was his daughter and wanted the privileges that came with being the daughter of a rich and powerful kingpin. In her young mind, she was thinking that Jesus would spoil her like her stepfather Alexandro did, even though Belen had told her that wouldn't be the case with him. He was a different breed of monster, and Belen was scared and cautious of him.

Belen gently took a hold of Fancy's hands across the table, the first motherly thing she'd done since the visit started, and looked into her daughter's eager eyes. She exhaled and coolly said, "Fancy, I know you're excited to meet with him, but he's not the man you think he's gonna be. He's a cold hearted monster and he doesn't care if you live or die. He will have you killed in a heartbeat for the slightest disrespect. And whatever you do, please do not acknowledge this man as your father when you meet with him."

Fancy was listening. She didn't respond right away.

"Promise me that, Fancy. Promise you will only see Jesus as your connect and not your father. He's a very dangerous man," Belen said with a bit of desperation in her tone.

Fancy stared at her mother and nodded. "I promise."

When Belen was satisfied with her daughter's reply, she said, "You are to go to the 34th Street heliport tomorrow. Arrangements have been made for you to travel to see him."

Fancy smiled slightly. She felt that she was more than ready. She was born to follow in her mother's footsteps and do it better than her. The family business was in her blood.

CHAPTER 2

The black Sloane helicopter flew through the crisp blue air like a stallion in the sky. It was the best way to travel in grandeur from New York to Pennsylvania. The occupants didn't have to worry about traffic or time; the sleek, black bird did up to a 100mph, moving fast like hurricane winds.

Fancy was cool and relaxed; traveling by plane and helicopter was familiar to her, but Nasir remained quiet and was nervous. This was something new to him. He had never been on a plane or helicopter, and a little airsickness started to churn in his stomach. He clutched Fancy's hand tightly without realizing he was doing it and sat still. He looked into space and prayed that gravity didn't go against them.

Fancy smiled at the odd gesture coming from Nasir and thought, *Fucking rookie.* Traveling by luxurious private jets and helicopters was how she used to get around in her old life with her parents. She remembered trips to the Hamptons by helicopter and trips abroad and around the country either by Learjet or first class.

It felt good to soar over the city once again, and finally be somewhere on time. The bird's-eye view from above was breathtaking. Fancy fixed her eyes on miles and miles of metropolis that suddenly altered into sprawling greenery, farmland, and thick trees. The landscape below had changed so suddenly, like they had gone through a portal. Arriving at their destination in Pennsylvania was going to be fast.

The two men seated in front of Fancy and Nasir were two of Jesus' henchmen. They were tall and harrowing figures clad in dark suits and wearing mirror sunglasses to hide the coldness in their eyes. They looked like killers more than businessmen in their sharp attire. Fancy noticed the holstered Desert Eagles underneath their black jackets. It was a serious piece of hardware—a powerful gun. The men's only job was to escort Fancy and Nasir from New York to the unknown location in Pennsylvania. The henchmen didn't make conversation or show any hospitality. It wasn't their job to make friends. If they had to, within the blink of an eye, they would shoot both Nasir and Fancy under orders from Jesus and toss their bodies out of the flying helicopter.

Everyone was quiet; the only thing heard was the sound of the helicopter moving through the sky. Fancy had so many things running through her mind. What would her father look like? Would he be as handsome and elegant as Alexandro? Would he embrace her with open arms and acknowledge that she was his daughter? Or would he be heartless, like a wild animal in the jungle? There were so many things to think, and also worry about. Belen was adamant that she not acknowledge that he was her father. The concern was stuck on Fancy like a foul smell. She felt trepidation as they came closer to the landing zone in the backwoods of Pennsylvania.

The helicopter started to descend. Fancy looked down at the opaque area of trees and wondered where they were going to land this bird. She didn't see any type of heliport for miles. Only thick, tall trees dominated the area. The helicopter came across an open grassy area on the ground, and parked below was a black Escalade.

When the Sloane helicopter finally touched the ground, the men slid the door open and immediately made their exit from the machine. Nasir and Fancy followed behind them. They were in the middle of nowhere, surrounded by trees and isolation. There was a man dressed in the same dark suit waiting for them outside of the Escalade. He remained unsmiling as they approached. They were ushered to the vehicle and climbed inside. Immediately, they were whisked away to a secluded meeting place.

"This some Godfather, CIA shit right here," Nasir said faintly.

Fancy agreed.

The Escalade was swallowed up by the dense trees while it traveled up a dirt road into the mountains. Fancy and Nasir were so nervous, it almost felt like they couldn't breathe. No one was saying a word to them, only instructing and ushering them from one place to the next. The driver remained quiet and focused on the road. He was skilled behind the wheel and maneuvered from one winding road to the next, penetrating the large vehicle deeper into the forest.

Nasir kept focused on everything around him, but it was hard to remember what road the driver took; they twisted and turned so much, it became confusing. The roads all looked the same. He wasn't in Kansas anymore. He rarely traveled outside of the city like this, and when he did, it was always about business. But this was something different for him, like some James Bond, Miami Vice type of scene he saw on TV. He tried to remain composed, but his heart was beating a million times per second. What if they didn't make it back home alive? It could be a setup. But then, he had to think, why go through all of this movement for a setup when, with the power Jesus had, he could have easily had them killed in New York? He looked at Fancy, but she was also clueless.

They arrived fifteen minutes later at a sprawling log cabin on a mountaintop overlooking miles of land that seemed to go on continuously. Parked near the discreet log cabin were a line of dark SUVs and several armed men that stood everywhere, guarding the area. They carried machine guns and automatic weapons and looked like a fierce, killing detail.

Fancy and Nasir gulped hard. They had never seen anything like it. It was just like in the movies. It looked like they were about to meet with the President of the United States. The Escalade doors opened, a thin man gruffly instructed, "Out!" and once again they were escorted out and ushered toward the cabin. Surrounded by goons, Fancy exhaled and followed behind the thin man who seemed to be the one in charge. He was clad in a gray Armani suit and had a cattish look about him.

Fancy and Nasir were searched for weapons once more before they could take a step inside. When they entered the cabin, they marveled at the opulence displayed. It seemed like they had gone from the wilderness to a room at the Trump Towers. There were mahogany walls and ambient lighting providing a radiant glow. The place also featured a few abstract paintings, silver candlestick-shaped lamps, plus sleek chrome and marble-top coffee tables adorned with crystal bowls. The chandelier above was impressive, looking like diamond crystals hanging from above.

"Wow!" Fancy uttered.

Money could do and buy you anything, even give you a piece of luxury in the heart of a dense forest in a remote location.

The cattish-looking man turned to look at Fancy. He had no emotions. She was his only business, not Nasir; Nasir might as well been invisible to him. He stood erect and exuded importance.

"Jesus will meet with you in the next room," he said.

Fancy nodded.

This was it. She was about to come face to face with her real father. Fancy tried to control her emotions and her excitement. She didn't want to look desperate and come off as some naive and lost little girl to him.

"What about me?" Nasir asked.

The man cut his eyes at Nasir. "You are of no importance to Jesus."

His words displeased Nasir, but he was in no position to argue or fight with anyone.

The man looked at Fancy again. "And by the way, my name is Felipe Duarte. I am Jesus' right-hand man." His voice was cool, and his eyes showed calmness, even though Fancy read there was a killer behind them.

He ushered Fancy into the next room while Nasir was left waiting by the bar area. Nasir was fuming inside. He'd come so far and still wasn't allowed to see one of the most powerful men in the drug world. He watched Fancy disappear behind Felipe into the private room that was guarded by two armed thugs.

Fancy stepped into the coolness of the room. The decor was simplified with more abstract paintings and leather furniture. There weren't any amenities like a TV, radio or anything else—only books that lined the bookshelves. A man stood by the window behind a large oak desk, gazing at the outside with his back turned to them. His statuesque form was attractively tall and defined in an Italian suit.

"Jesus, this is Fancy," Felipe announced.

"I already know who she is, Felipe," Jesus responded coolly, without turning to acknowledge them. He continued to gaze outside; something out the window had his attention. He wasn't in any rush to meet her.

"Step outside, Felipe, and let us talk alone." Jesus' voice was commanding and strong. He was a man who didn't like to repeat himself.

"Yes, boss." Felipe walked out the room, closing the door behind him.

Fancy stood silently, her eyes transfixed on the man by the window. She was aching for him to turn around, so she could see his face—see if she resembled some likeness of him. She didn't want to move and she didn't want to give off the wrong impression. First impressions matter greatly, and she wanted to come off strong and mature to her father. But she remembered from her mother not to call him her father, but look at this as a meeting with her connect.

"You've come a long way, have you?" Jesus said lightly.

"I have," Fancy quickly answered.

"I'm not meaning in your travel, but in your way of life."

"Yes, I have, and I want to continue to grow," she replied calmly. She wanted to show Jesus that she was smart.

"From now on, we will refer to each other as colors," said Jesus.

Fancy was listening.

Jesus finally turned around to see the young girl face to face. She was beautiful. She stood before him in a white Capri set that accentuated her womanly curves, and wedged heels. Her long black hair gracefully fell down to her shoulders. She looked angelic and so innocent, not the type of woman he had been hearing things about.

Jesus was a handsome man with bronze skin and tapered salt and pepper hair and a corresponding thick goatee. He had manicured nails and short, cropped hair, and he reminded Fancy of Alexandro. Both men had style and class, and when they walked into a room, their presence was immediately known.

"I will refer to you as Rojo, which means red. And you will refer to me as Negro," he said to her.

Fancy nodded, and uttered, "Rojo."

Jesus moved himself from the window and behind his desk and walked toward Fancy. His steps were small, but powerful, and his gaze was icy. He looked Fancy up and down silently. He liked what he saw. Fancy stood like a statue before him. Being in the presence of one of the most powerful men in the world sent butterflies swimming around in her stomach. It was nerve-racking. With the snap of his fingers, Jesus could control if she lived or died—if she became wealthy or not. He was like a god in her eyes.

He had a Colombian accent, but he spoke English really well. He seemed so reserved at first.

"Are you hungry, thirsty?" Jesus asked her.

"I'm okay."

Jesus went over to his oak desk and flipped open a long, handcrafted casing filled with Cuban cigars. He removed one. He turned to look at Fancy and asked, "Do you smoke?"

"Not cigars," she responded respectfully.

"You are missing out. Cigars are flavorsome and help you think and relax." Jesus said.

Jesus placed the cigar between his lips, sliced the tip off with a cigar cutter, and lit it. He took a few pulls from the succulent tobacco and exhaled. He removed the cigar from his lips and examined it like it needed inspection.

"Two things I love in this world, a good cigar and fine wine."

"I understand."

Jesus approached her. "Do I make you nervous?"

Yes, he did. But Fancy didn't want to look weak. She remained pokerfaced and still.

"No."

"But you have heard about my pedigree?"

"Yes."

He smiled. "And what is my name?" he asked with a profound stare at her.

Fancy was about to utter "Jesus," but she quickly remembered what he wanted to be called. "Negro."

"I like that. You listen, you understand."

I am your daughter, she thought.

Jesus took a few more drags from the cigar and then said, "Belen wishes for you to have more responsibility. That, I will grant to you. I've been watching and observing you, and you seem to have proven yourself."

"Thank you."

"You thank me and you don't know what I'm about to offer you."

"Whatever it is, I know I can handle it, Mr. Negro. I was born to do this, carry on in my mother's footsteps." It was the most Fancy had said since the meeting.

He gazed at her—always sizing up the young, beautiful girl. She was really young, but he would give her a chance.

"I want you to take over certain aspects of my organization," he mentioned.

Fancy perked up. She was excited about the prospect of working directly with Jesus. She continued to keep her composure, though, while he explained the operation.

"Amarillo, whom you will meet soon, operates the Miami shorelines, and oversees the boats of freight coming from Colombia to Miami. Once the product is received, it will get to New York, where you, Rojo, will head up the northern region of my organization. You will distribute the product through New York, Pennsylvania, Virginia, D.C, Maryland, South Carolina and North Carolina," Jesus proclaimed.

Fancy was elated that she was chosen to head up such a large chunk of the organization. She wanted to run and give her father a hug for trusting her, but once again, she remembered her mother's words. She kept herself glued to the same spot she has been standing at.

"I won't let you down, Mr. Negro," Fancy said with assurance.

"I know you won't. Because if you let me down, not only will I murder you, but I will surely slaughter your family and your family's family. We have rules, here, Rojo; rules that you must abide by. If you steal from us, we kill you. If you get arrested and decide to snitch, we kill you, your mother, and your kids, and will make it look like you never existed. If you try to go against the cartel in any way, you are a dead woman," Jesus said.

Fancy gulped hard. Her heart sank into her stomach. Jesus' eyes were a chilling cold against her. She soon realized that she was just another employee to him—expendable. She never once questioned why he suddenly decided to bring her into his world. The only thing Fancy thought about was being wealthy, with endless power, and proving to everyone that she could do and be better than her parents. She wanted to run New York City.

Jesus continued to school her about the rules and the organization. She was drilled about talking on phones and where to drop the money to be laundered. She had assassins at her beck and call when dealing with Jesus and became aware that they ran their cartel like a business and knew how to stay one step ahead of the government.

This was it, the big leagues, and there was no turning back. She had asked for this chance, and now that it was in front of her face, she refused to be intimidated by it and fuck it up.

"You are in my world now, little girl, and this is grown man business. There is no retirement plan from this, no 401(k), just lots of money being made and chances," Jesus said gruffly. "And sometimes chances don't work out for everyone."

For a moment, Fancy's knees began to buckle slightly and she became clammy, but she continued to stand tall. She thought to herself, if her mother could do it, then so could she.

CHAPTER 3

The sprawling Long Island Cemetery in Farmingdale, New York was well manicured with rich green grass, cared-for graves, and stillness. Fancy gazed at the granite headstone embedded into the grass and soil; ALEXANDRO J. LANE was etched into the fine stone, marking his final resting place. Fancy felt ambivalent about so many things happening in her life, especially the meeting with Jesus. He gave her a chilling feeling. Alexandro would have never been so coldhearted and aloof toward her. He truly loved her. But Jesus, he was a different story. He was a malicious being of power and coldness that could spread like a virus in her life. There had to be a good reason why Belen kept her in the dark for so long and Jesus out of her life. But greed and power made Fancy yearn to get closer to him.

Fancy stood over the grave of the man she had thought was her father for a long time, with the cold winter air nipping at her skin and a few tears trickling down her cheeks. Wrapped snuggly in her mink coat and knee-high boots, she closed her eyes and thought about the good times for a moment. They were fun and lasting. However, she couldn't help but become emotional and sad. The FBI raid, the sudden truth about family and friends, and the trials and tribulations she endured came into her mind like a bad nightmare. Abruptly losing everything she grew up around, and what her parents hustled hard for, was still a devastating feeling. But standing at the burial site of Alexandro, was the last thing she expected to happen. Alexandro was once a powerful and respected man, and she watched him crumble easily like paper and fade into this disgraceful memory.

Despite Alexandro not being her biological pops, she still loved him greatly and had a strong connection with him. It was hard to believe that he was gone. And it was harder to believe that her mother, his wife, was behind his demise. Fancy clutched the bouquet of flowers in her hand. They were for him. She wanted Alexandro to know that whatever truth was revealed, he would never be forgotten and would always be loved.

She crouched down beside her father's grave and placed the flowers against his headstone. A few more tears fell from her eyes as she stared at the name. How would people remember him? She knew how she would remember him; despite what the media and everyone else was saying about her father, he was still a good man. Fancy so badly wanted to feel his protection. She wanted to feel his masculine arms wrap around her like a warm blanket and hear from him that everything was going to be okay. She needed to hear his advice and have him by her side during these trying times. She was learning about the streets on her own—surviving, and educating herself about a world he so desperately tried to separate her from. But this way of life was inevitable, she felt. Fancy knew he would have been so proud of her. She wanted to represent her daddy in the game.

"I came a long way, Pop-Pop," she said faintly. "I wish you could see your little princess now."

She rested her hand against the headstone and closed her eyes again. She took a deep breath and exhaled. She wanted to spread out and lie next to him. The solitude in the cold gave her minor comfort. For some strange reason, she felt safe there—shielded from any danger. The frost in her lungs allowed her to breathe again.

Fancy lingered at her father's gravesite for an hour. She talked to him like he was there, listening. Her BMW was parked in the cemetery, out of the public view, and she kept her .380 close at all times. She was aware that she had made enemies coming up in this business, and the one thing she learned best was to always be alert and expect the unexpected. When her mother put a hit out on her own husband, it made Fancy realize that even your own flesh and blood wasn't to be trusted. She understood the saying: Keep your friends close and your enemies closer.

Her relationship with Nasir was still steady and going, but she sensed some hints of jealousy with him and felt some turbulence, especially after her meeting with Jesus. Nasir was bitter that she met with him alone. He wanted to see the boss of all bosses, and the fact that he was one room away and was still denied the chance made him upset.

When Fancy walked out of the room after her meeting with Jesus, Nasir's attitude had changed. He frowned heavily and was silent toward Fancy, like she was the one who had done him wrong. Fancy noticed his childish attitude and chose to ignore it. They had left the remote compound in silence, and the way they arrived was the same way they departed.

They had arrived in New York late that evening. Fancy understood the instructions that were given to her from the cartel. Overnight, she had become the HBIC, "head bitch in charge," and her position wasn't going to sit well with so many people, especially the men in the game.

Nasir was the first one to show his displeasure with the new arrangement and power position she was thrust into. How the fuck did she have control over the northern region? It was power Nasir always dreamed of having. But his little fake cousin done pulled the rug from underneath him and stood over him.

"What makes you so fuckin' special, huh, Fancy?" he had argued.

"Nasir, I didn't ask for this. It came unexpectedly," she had replied.

"If it wasn't for me, you wouldn't even be in the game. I started you. I made you," he had griped strongly.

Fancy had frowned. Yeah, he started her in the game, but Fancy perfected the hustle. It was in her blood. And it wasn't too long ago that Nasir had left her out to dry, played her and used her—made her kill a child, took advantage of her and left her penniless while he was eating like a fat cat. Now the shoe was on the other foot. What goes around, comes around. And now she was like cream—rising to the top.

Nasir could cry foul all he wanted, but the referees were on her side and she controlled the game.

"You are still in this with me, Nasir. Look at us, we can run this fuckin' city. I just need you to love me and be by my side. You are my right hand," Fancy said to him.

Nasir didn't respond. He was too blinded by his ego to see a good thing in front of him.

"And why wouldn't he meet with me?" he had exclaimed.

Fancy didn't have a legitimate answer for him. If a man like Jesus didn't want to meet with you, then he didn't.

"I don't know."

"I don't give fuck who he is, the nigga bleeds just like everyone else," he had added, talking insane.

Fancy couldn't explain to him that Jesus was really her biological father. She was warned not to tell anyone about it, even the ones closest to her. But the look in Nasir's eyes was a frightening one. Fancy figured he would get over it, because soon, they both would be making too much money to be bitter about anything.

Their ride back to Brooklyn was a sour one. Nasir remained quiet. Fancy wanted to remain focused. The minute they touched into their Brooklyn hood, Nasir made himself ghost by jumping into his midnight-black CLS63 Benz and racing off without saying goodbye. He left Fancy feeling somewhat dubious about many things. There was too much at stake for anyone to fuck it up . . . even when it came to love.

Fancy said her final goodbyes to her father. She dried her tears and had a heavy heart.

"Goodbye, Pop-Pop. I will always love you, and I will continue to make you proud and carry on with the Lane family name with respect and pride," she said tearfully.

She stood erect and began her way toward her car. The cold winter wind cut into her soul with her heart becoming icy, and the murder of her father was a chilling reminder that there wasn't any room for mistakes. The drug game didn't come with second chances and restart buttons.

Fancy climbed into her car and sighed heavily. This new era in her life had her in the fast lane and she had to keep up with the other sports cars doing a 100-plus on the freeway.

Fancy looked at herself in the rearview mirror and held her own stare. She said to herself, "There's no room for any errors."

CHAPTER 4

Miami, Florida

"Él es un idiota," Esmeralda said uncouthly, causing the other ladies to erupt with laughter in her beauty salon. "He's a dumb muthafucka and she's a dumb bitch for even fuckin' wit' that puto!"

"Esmeralda, leave her man alone. She didn't know," one of the beauticians replied in good humor.

"No, she's a fuckin' idiot, too, Miranda. I'm sayin', they fuckin' deserve each other, they're both are fools . . . culero!"

"She ain't even here to defend herself."

"What that bitch needs to defend herself from is that stupid muthafucka. I think Tina's slow and shit. I mean, don't she look it? Bitch always coming in here lookin' like a character out of Sesame Street . . . ella no tiene ninguna style . . . and her pussy is probably as wide as the Grand Canyon."

The beauty shop filled with ladies laughed again at Esmeralda's sharp tongue.

"Girl, you ain't got no shame," said one of the customers sitting in the chair getting a relaxer.

"I just tell it like it is, and if they don't like it, then fuck 'em," Esmeralda replied.

KIM K.

She brought about good, harsh humor in her own beauty salon, located in the heart of Little Havana, home to many Cuban immigrant residents, as well as many residents from Central and South America. Esmeralda's salon and spa, a multicultural hair salon, was always lively and filled with loyal clientele that always came her way to get their hair professionally done. The decor was top-notch—two flat-screen TVs mounted on both sides of the walls so the ladies could be entertained by their daily soap operas or reality shows. The waiting area was lined with the softest couches, up-to-date magazines spread across the glass coffee tables and snacks for people to munch on as they waited for their beautician to call for them.

Esmeralda's clientele ranged from her own kind—all the Hispanic girls, Dominican, Colombian, Puerto Rican—to some African Americans and a sprinkle of female Caucasians that came from South Beach or other posh areas in Miami to get their hair treated by one of the best in the city. They took the risk of traveling into the hood to Esmeralda's shop—Hair Xtreme. Her shop was popular in the low-income neighborhood and it gave her workers a decent living. She had a staff of up to six loyal hair stylists who loved her. She was witty, raw and blunt with her words, but her brash way of thinking and approach was what everyone loved about Esmeralda. She was that bitch who always told it like it was, in Spanish or in English, however you wanted to hear it, whether you liked it or not. And she didn't have any family, so her workers were her family.

The salon had a small kitchen in the back where she had her peoples cooking their beans and rice, along with plantains and other Latino dishes, and she would feed it to her customers or to anyone who was hungry. It was that kind of thinking that made everyone flock to her and made her truly loved.

Esmeralda was a twenty-six-year old immigrant from Colombia. She came to America with her parents when she was five years old, and soon became a United States citizen. Her stunning beauty was hypnotizing; sometimes it was hard to believe that such an attractive woman—who stood five-eight, with defined legs that stretched to the heavens, dark olive skin, a shape like a video vixen, and high cheekbones, her face surrounded by straight, sun-bleached blonde shiny tresses—had a mouth like a sailor on her.

Most times it was curses and ranting. Everyone got used to her vile tongue. She had grown up really poor in Colombia, and some knew her story of how she strived, fought hard, and started up her own business in time frame that appeared to be overnight.

But Esmeralda had a dirty little secret that she kept hidden like a bastard child in the 1920s. The bulk of her income was made from distributing cocaine. She had some harrowing Miami connections and even though her shop was legit, it was also a front for other, shady revenue. Unbeknownst to everyone, Esmeralda would watch the drug dealers come to pick up their girlfriends from her shop in expensive cars and sparkly jewelry, and see them flash wads of hundreds to pay for their girls' hair, and she would call up her goons to rob them when possible. Her goons would follow the men far enough away so that her shop wasn't implicated in the robbery. It was easy money and it had been going on for months.

Esmeralda was watching one particular woman get her hair done in the booth across from hers this sunny evening. Sandy was doing a silk fusion on a drug dealer's girlfriend; her name was Kim, and her boyfriend's name was Whiz. He was big in Miami and in South Beach. Whiz ran with a fierce crew who called themselves, "The Ghost Ridas" and his main chick enjoyed all the fruits of his hard labor. Esmeralda continued to talk, while putting a perm in her client's hair.

"All I'm saying is bitches like us need to be better . . . fuck I look like letting some lame puto get between my legs and take a bite out of my precious cookie? Shit, he gonna have to work for this pussy, y'all feel me?"

said Esmeralda harshly as she subtly eyed Kim in the next chair with her face buried in a Vibe magazine. Kim wasn't paying her any attention, but Esmeralda was sizing her up.

Esmeralda fixed her eyes on Kim's coral John Galliano halter summer dress. The drug dealer's wifey was bejeweled in platinum and diamonds; judging from her David Yurman diamond hoop earrings, 5-karat diamond tennis bracelet, 10-karat white gold and the diamond encrusted ring, along with the Chopard watch she sported — the bitch was paid. And Esmeralda wanted everything that bitch had on. It was time for another setup.

The evening progressed and Esmeralda was done with her client's hair. The client paid cash and was thankful for the outcome. When the woman left, Esmeralda walked over to Sandy. She was almost done touching up Kim's hair.

"You almost done with her, Sandy?" she asked.

Sandy nodded.

"And are you good? You need anything?" Esmeralda asked Kim.

Kim didn't pay Esmeralda any attention. She kept busy texting on her iPhone, and she acted like nobody existed to her. It seemed like everything else was more important than her surroundings. Esmeralda and her raggedy shop were unimportant. She was a pretentious bitch, and Esmeralda knew her type. They got with a big shot drug dealer, lived a fraction of the good life because they spread their legs and gave a nigga with money some good head, and now they acted like their shit didn't stink.

Esmeralda kept her cool. She smiled and walked away. It was getting late and it was almost time for her salon to close. Kim and another African American female were the only ones still getting their hair done. Most of the crowd had gone, and the liveliness and laughter in the shop had faded—gone until tomorrow. The flat screens had been turned off, and a young female worker started to sweep up around the shop. Esmeralda went into her back-room office and closed the door. She removed her cell phone from her smock and dialed a familiar number. It rang a few times, and a male's raspy voice answered.

"Hey, holla at me, Esmeralda," said the man in a lively tone.

"I got something for you," she said.

"That's what I need to hear. What you got?"

"This bitch in my shop stunting with jewels and shines. And I know who her man is," she said.

"Oh word? That's what's up. I'm down to get wit' that," Rise replied.

"Hurry though, Rise. Sandy's touching up a few loose ends on her head and I know her man is gonna be around to come get her soon."

"Who her man?" he asked.

"Whiz."

"Word, we been tryin' to get at that nigga for months now. I know that nigga is bankin'. We gonna be 'round in a few, do what you can to stall that bitch," the man said.

He hung up. The setup had been put into motion.

Esmeralda walked out of her office with a smile and a cool demeanor. She said a few words to her workers and walked outside her shop to smoke a cigarette. The Miami air was temperate. Esmeralda took a few pulls from the Newport she smoked and looked around. She was ruthless and on a mission. She was a bitch about her money, but at the same time, she wanted to keep a low profile. She knew killers, thugs, kingpins and notorious drug dealers. They all yearned to fuck her, but Esmeralda, even though she loved dick, had a special someone in her life, and her name was Sexy. Sexy was finally back home from New York, which she traveled back and forth to continuously.

After a long day at the shop, the only thing Esmeralda wanted to do was go home, shed away her clothing, take a nice, hot shower and nestle with her chick and make passionate love to her. Sexy was a light-skinned black female from Brooklyn, who had just been released from MCC, Metropolitan Correctional Center, in New York. The two fell in love and became an item. Together, they were a dangerous couple.

Esmeralda made a call home and had a brief conversation with Sexy. It had been a week since she'd seen Sexy and she missed her greatly. But as she spoke, her two-way chimed in; it was Rise calling back. She put Sexy on hold and answered the call.

"Yeah," she said.

"Yo, we be there in ten minutes, that bitch still there, right?" the male goon uttered.

"Yeah, but I don't think she's gonna be ten minutes long," said Esmeralda.

"Stall that bitch. Her man there yet?" Rise asked.

Esmeralda looked up and down the block. She didn't see his car. "No."

"Good. We on our way."

He hung up and Esmeralda returned to her conversation with Sexy.

"I miss you, baby," she said.

"I miss you, too. When you comin' home?" Sexy asked in her soothing voice.

"Soon. I just gotta handle a little more business and then I'm all yours tonight."

"Don't be too long."

"I won't."

Esmeralda hung up the call and walked back into the shop. Kim was done. She was already on her phone calling her man. Esmeralda walked up to Kim and decided to give her a compliment on her wardrobe and style.

"Girl, I love those shoes," she said.

Kim remained deadpan. "Thanks."

"Where did you get them from?"

"They expensive and my man bought them for me," Kim replied matter-of-factly.

Kim showed off a smug look. She was short with her reply and looked like she didn't want to be bothered with anyone.

Esmeralda wanted to smack the snobbism and attitude out of that bitch. She knew she came from the Pork 'n' Beans projects, and now this bitch wanted to act like she was born into money and royalty.

Kim started to collect her things and leave. Esmeralda didn't want to look too suspicious, so she didn't interfere with her leaving. She just hoped that Rise was almost there. She wanted this bitch to get got for everything she owned. Esmeralda's workers also noticed Kim's snobbish attitude and frowned. That stuck-up bitch didn't even leave a decent tip for Sandy after she'd spent several hours working on her nappy hair. It was all good. Esmeralda planned on compensating Sandy for the bullshit she had to put up with by sliding her a couple dollars after they liquidated Kim's jewels.

She watched Kim leave abruptly when the midnight-black Audi A7 sitting on spinning, chromed rims pulled up to the salon. Esmeralda knew it was Whiz. The windows were tinted and rap music was heard blaring. A six-two Hispanic male bejeweled in more gold and platinum than Mr. T stepped out from the driver's side with his long chains swinging and a hard scowl, rocking a mini Afro. Whiz was handsome and well known in the game.

Kim was suddenly all smiles.

"Hey baby," she greeted warmly while throwing her arms around her man to give him a nice welcoming hug.

They kissed briefly. Esmeralda watched everything from the floor of her shop. Whiz observed his surroundings quickly, as a true cautious hustler should always do and looked into the shop. He locked eyes with Esmeralda and frowned.

"You good, baby?" Whiz asked his woman.

"Yeah, I'm good, let's just go. I wanna go out tonight," she replied.

They both jumped into the Audi A7. Esmeralda began to worry, thinking she was going to miss out on a golden opportunity. Rise hadn't shown up yet. But just when Esmeralda was about to give up hope, her cell phone rang. She quickly answered and heard Rise say, "Yo quickly, that's them gettin' into the black Audi A7?"

"Yes, it is."

"A'ight, we on them."

Esmeralda hung up, relieved that they showed up on time. She walked to the door and observed Rise behind the wheel of a black Chevy Impala with a few of his goons. There were two cars behind the Audi and ready to make their move when they were farther away from the shop. She smiled and pulled out another cigarette to smoke. The next phone call she expected was from Rise telling her that the robbery was successful.

Rise followed behind the Audi A7 closely. He wasn't trying to bring too much suspicion on himself. He knew Whiz was a dangerous gangster who was always armed. He wanted the stickup to go as smoothly as possible, but if it came down to it, then Rise wouldn't hesitate to shoot down both occupants in the car and go about his business.

The Audi traveled South down SW 27th Avenue on the busy street of Little Havana. Rise's occupants locked and loaded their automatic weapons and had the ski masks ready to put on. This was a familiar scene to them. The thrill of catching niggas slipping in Miami was like being in some sweet pussy—it made niggas hard.

"Yo, y'all muthafuckas ready? I've been lookin' to catch this nigga for months now. Be on point," said Rise.

"We on this nigga, Rise . . . fo' real," the passenger replied.

They followed the couple from block to block and turn after turn, waiting for the right moment to strike. They already knew that his chick was loaded with jewels, and now it was time to hit 'em up.

Rise saw his chance when the Audi made a right onto a dimly lit street into the bad neighborhood and came to a stop at a red light. He accelerated and maneuvered the Impala in front of the Audi, blocking it from going any farther, and before Whiz could make a move, reaching underneath his seat for his gun, a .44 Magnum was shoved against his temple and he heard the frightful sound of, "Nigga, if you move fuckin' wrong, I'll blow ya fuckin' brains out!"

The two men came out of nowhere, looming from the darkness. Kim screeched, but she was told to shut the fuck up. Before they knew it, four men in ski masks surrounded the vehicle with their automatic weapons. Whiz frowned heavily. The diamond necklace was snatched from around Kim's neck. She tried to resist, but was met with a quick fist to her face that spewed blood from her nose. Whiz tried to react, but he was met with a quick pistol whipping, and then came the instructions.

"You follow orders, and maybe y'all live. You don't, we gonna lullaby both y'all asses within a heartbeat," the alpha male growled.

Whiz was defenseless. The side of his face was bruised, and he didn't see himself getting out of this situation alive. They made Kim exit the car and ride in the Chevy, while two men rode with Whiz. It was simple: Take them to his stash house without any problems and his girl would live. If he resisted, they were both dead. Whiz reluctantly agreed to do so. With a .44 pressed to the back of his head, he led the way to his place.

"Remember, just follow fuckin' instructions 'n' we all gonna get through this the easy way," said the man holding the pistol behind his head.

KIM K.

Esmeralda pulled up to the high-rise, thirty-five-story building on Brickell Avenue. It was late and she was tired. She parked in the underground garage and stepped out of her powder-blue BMW, with her stilettos touching the concrete and her hand near the pistol concealed on her person. In her line of work, she couldn't afford to take any chances. She pushed for the elevator to take her up to her luxurious apartment on the twenty-fifth floor, but before she stepped inside, her cell phone rang. Seeing that it was Rise calling, she answered right away, eager to hear some good news.

"Que?" she answered.

"It went down," Rise mentioned.

"Good to hear. And the take?" Esmeralda asked with a smile.

"Really good, but there was one problem."

"And the problem was?"

"That bitch will no longer be needing her hair done at ya shop, and Whiz is officially retired," Rise said coolly.

Esmeralda knew what he was saying, without trying to say it; they both were dead. She hadn't sanctioned the hit and became furious with Rise.

"Rise, I didn't ask for this," she exclaimed.

"I know, but shit happens, and it went down suddenly."

They both were saying too much over the phone. Esmeralda was raised to speak about murders and business matters only in person. Fearing too much was already said, she hung up the call and sighed heavily. She would deal with Rise later on.

The elevator lifted like a slingshot into the air and Esmeralda ascended to her floor. She stepped into the lavishly decorated hallway of the sky-rise residence and proceeded to her apartment. When she stepped into her dimly lit apartment, the first thing she did was kick off her heels. She shouted out, "Baby, I'm home," and went out onto the balcony.

Esmeralda took in a deep breath and admired the picturesque view from her position. The final thing she needed was a glass of wine in her hand.

"Hey baby," Esmeralda heard.

She turned around to see Sexy approaching her, clad in a baby-doll top and matching thong, along with a pair of six-inch stilettos. Sexy was too enticing. A wide smile formed across Esmeralda's face.

Sexy was holding two glasses of white wine in her hands and stepped out onto the balcony to greet her lover.

"I missed you," said Esmeralda.

"I missed you too, baby."

The two kissed passionately for a moment. Sexy broke away from her lover and held Esmeralda's loving gaze. With the city of Miami painted in the background, it was the perfect getaway for both ladies growing up in harshness and depravity.

"How was New York?" Esmeralda asked.

"I acquired some important news that you might find very interesting."

"Like what?"

Sexy had many connects and people loyal to her up north. She knew Esmeralda's story of coming from Colombia and who her parents were. Esmeralda felt betrayed back in Colombia. And she had a deep hatred for one man and his family. She wanted to kill everything he loved and adored, or bred.

"I received word from a reliable source that Jesus has another child," Sexy informed her.

Hearing about another child of Jesus made Esmeralda's nostrils flare and caused her to clench her jaws.

"Where?" Esmeralda demanded to know.

"New York, and it's a girl."

Esmeralda was steaming; Jesus had killed those she loved, and she was trying to murder any and everyone connected to him. And it had become a daunting task. She wanted her revenge and she was going to get it, by executing everything in that man's family genes. From Colombia to the States, Esmeralda had hired a team of ruthless mercenaries to find Pablo. "She's either living in New York or New Jersey. That information is sketchy. Her name is Fancy and it appears that she's making quite a name for herself on the streets. Both of her parents were incarcerated, but now one is dead—the stepfather," Sexy informed her.

"I want that bitch dead," Esmeralda exclaimed.

"I understand, and the feeling is mutual. But I was thinking that we go at her with a different tactic," said Sexy. "Do things differently."

"Like how?"

Sexy showed off a deceitful grin, thinking about the master plan. She gazed at the city skyline for a minute and then turned her attention back to Esmeralda. She proclaimed, "Instead of murdering this bitch right away, we make friends with her."

"Friends?" Esmeralda spat with a twisted frown.

"Yes, Esmeralda. We get into her circle, allow this bitch to trust us, or you. We get in close enough so that it could lead us to Jesus, and then hopefully Pablo," Sexy proclaimed.

Esmeralda liked the idea so far.

Sexy continued, "With Fancy being Jesus' illegitimate child and not being raised under Jesus' tutelage, she would be less likely to die for her father than the others. If she's smart she'll give up the information. And if she doesn't know anything about Pablo or her father, she will die either way."

Esmeralda wanted to go along with the idea. It was smart and deceitful at the same time. She approved of it.

The two ladies raised their glasses filled with white wine and toasted. Tonight, they would celebrate for two reasons: One, Sexy was finally home and back in her lover's arms, and two, it would be the end of her enemies and she would have her revenge against Jesus and Pablo.

They wrapped themselves in each other's arms heatedly and kissed wildly. Slowly, Sexy's adjustable straps were peeled from her shoulders and fell against her arms. Esmeralda wanted to suck on her hard, pink nipples. She marveled at Sexy's beauty and needed to release some stress. And Sexy was the perfect remedy. The two engaged into a prolonged kiss on the balcony, their tongues finding and wrestling with each other. Esmeralda slid her hand between her lovers' legs and pressed the palm of her hand against her sweet mound. Soon, Esmeralda was stripping naked on the balcony, freeing herself from the restriction of her clothing and Sexy continued to peel away her scanty attire. They continued to kiss and fondle each other.

The two lovers found themselves on the living room floor. Sexy lay on her back, and Esmeralda climbed on top of her, pressing her naked body into hers. Sexy spread her legs and Esmeralda made dessert out of her luscious tits, licking and sucking on Sexy's hardened nipples. Sexy anticipated Esmeralda going down on her, and that she did, kissing her way down to Sexy's stomach and positioning herself between her thick thighs. Esmeralda took her fingers and spread Sexy's pussy lips softly and gently, then licked her clit, working her tongue up inside her lover and thrusting fingers into her until Sexy was squirming and moaning. She held her mouth against Sexy's wet slit and ate and ate until a river of juices flowed against her mouth. Sexy was ready to cum in her mouth.

The two changed position and it was time for Esmeralda to feel the effects of a wicked tongue lashing between her legs. Sexy alternated between driving her tongue in her pussy and in her ass, causing Esmeralda to reach back and spread her ass cheeks wider so Sexy could completely do her magic. Esmeralda grinded her pussy into Sexy's face with zeal.

The ladies enjoyed each other for an hour, flipping each other around until their pussies were against each other, becoming locked into the scissor position. They could feel the heat of each other's warm wetness of their slippery folds. They scissored their legs with one another and started bumping and grinding heavily, rubbing clit to clit, sharing juices and passion, and feeling the strong signs of an orgasm approaching. And within time, they both bathed each other in their sweet honey. Esmeralda exploded first and the powerful feeling sent her over the edge. Sexy came seconds afterwards, and she jerked and quivered, with her body glowing from the aftermath.

After the intense sexual session, the two curled up into each other's arms and lay against the floor for a moment. They continued to fondle each other and talk, just basking in the glow of something so good.

Sexy locked eyes with Esmeralda. "I will kill anything for you, baby. You just point and they're toe-tagged. I love you that much."

Esmeralda smiled. "I love you, too, baby."

They shared another deep kiss and fell asleep where they had just finished fucking. The next day, flight arrangements would be made to fly into New York, and the hunt to find Fancy would begin.

CHAPTER 5

Nasir's black CLS63 Benz sat parked discreetly in the backstreets of Brooklyn. The radio was playing low, and he was very familiar with the urban block he was parked on. With his tinted windows and under the cover of night, he wasn't worried about any interruptions. The pistol was near his reach, but he wasn't thinking about any danger at the moment. Nasir reclined in his seat. He closed his eyes and groaned loudly. The luscious, full lips wrapped around his fat dick gave him a temporary escape from everything that was going on in his crazy world. His hand was entwined in the long, black hair weave of the girl who was curved over in the front seat with her face deep in Nasir's lap. She sucked his dick like a porn star, while he reached around her curvy figure and finger popped her pulsating pussy.

He felt her juices saturating his fingers while he concentrated on the task at hand, thrusting, pumping, and driving his hard dick into her wet mouth. It felt like wet sex. The pretty-faced, brown-eyed young girl slobbered him down with saliva and grunts.

"Yes, do that shit . . . do that shit for Daddy!" Nasir moaned. He gripped the back of the girl's head and forced her face farther into his lap, causing her to deep throat his big dick. She didn't gag a bit.

She rolled his balls around in her fingers and explored his growing erection farther with her tongue. Nasir squirmed a little against the leather seat. His pants were around his ankles and he threw the moon roof back to let a little air circulate inside the car. It was getting hot and heavy inside.

The young, sultry, big-breasted girl licked and sucked him all over. Nasir was hers for the moment and she wanted to please him by any means necessary. She was familiar with his rapidly growing reputation in the streets. She also knew about his girlfriend, Fancy. But Fancy wasn't a concern for either of them tonight—tonight it was about busting a great nut from the blowjob being performed on him.

Nasir continued to moan and groan. She was the best he ever had. Fancy couldn't suck dick like her, not even on her best day. He needed some really sloppy head, where a bitch wasn't concerned about his pre-cum or shooting his load inside her mouth and having her swallow. She was just nasty with it, and he loved every moment of it.

She continued to please him with her wet, gaping mouth by sliding her soft, full lips down his shaft and back again. She looked up at Nasir with a smile and wink. He felt his knees shaking a bit as she continued with the method—her nice lips going up and down on his thick dick. She sucked harder, trying to pull the cum from his dick. She was showing him that he may be the boss on the streets, but at this moment, she was in control.

Nasir's pre-cum was leaking and his dick was throbbing inside her mouth. She took his dick, with the head of his penis deep in her throat.

"Damn baby . . . oh shit, damn, don't fuckin' stop, don't stop…it feels so good. It feels so good, so good . . ." he chanted.

She paused her nasty action and uttered, "Nasir, I want you to cum in my mouth."

"I will, baby . . . I fuckin' will," he grunted.

Nasir closed his eyes and relished in the moment. For a brief moment, he felt paradise. He had a lot to think about and had a lot going on. He wasn't sitting well with Fancy's newfound position in the game. He was finding it hard to relinquish power not only to his girl—the one he trained and brought into the game—but to the cartel that was now running things, which meant they were probably running his life too. But Nasir refused to be bullied by anyone, no matter who the fuck they were. It also bothered him that he'd traveled all that way to the backwoods of Pennsylvania and wasn't allowed to see Jesus. He felt like someone's doormat—unimportant.

He saw things changing and they were changing fast, and if he didn't react, then he was gonna lose out. He wanted to be the boss man—the one having the access and connect with Jesus, but somehow Fancy was granted that status. Nasir knew he had to be careful, that getting into bed with any cartel could be hazardous to your health—meaning one fuckup, no matter how small, and they could be finding pieces of you scattered across the Tri-State area for months.

But Nasir was a gangster and he was bred to be the best at hustling. He didn't scare frequently or easily. He would show the cartel that if push came to shove, then he wasn't going to be anything nice to mess with. The cartel was a crew of ruthless thugs, and Nasir wanted to prove that he could be just as ruthless.

He grunted again, and could feel the cum in his nuts boiling up as shorty continued to suck his dick like a professional. Moments like this one were good things. He was close to eruption. She sucked his dick, licked it, swallowed it like a tasty meal, and wanted to feel his creamy, white semen go down her throat. He chanted and moaned, thrusting upwards, shoving more dick into her throat. His fingers continued to slide inside her pink, wet folds. The sloppy, wet blowjob was making Nasir's eyes flutter.

"Oh shit! I'm gonna cum!" he cried out.

Her lips worked faster and harder around his dick.

Nasir grabbed her weave and then filled his hand with her full breasts, kneading them softly and pinching her hardened nipples. He huffed and puffed and spread his legs wider.

"I'm fuckin' coming!" he shouted.

She licked, sucked, and licked some more. She was ready to feel him shoot his warm, sticky load into her mouth. She wanted to taste him. She wanted to feel his release slide down her throat and fill her belly with his seed. It wouldn't be too long. Nasir fucked her mouth and she deep throated, and then suddenly, he grunted and vibrated, and exploded inside her mouth. She consumed every last drop of his sperm as Nasir fell back against the driver seat out of pure exhaustion. He whimpered like a baby— but was truly satisfied like a man. She wiped her mouth and smiled.

He didn't have time to lie around and dwell on a good nut. He was a busy man.

"Hurry up and put ya clothes back on," he said to her.

Nasir pulled up his jeans and fastened them. As he did so, his cell phone started to ring. He looked at the caller I.D to see who was calling, and it was Fancy.

"Don't say one fuckin' word," Nasir warned the young girl.

She nodded.

He answered, "What's up, babe?"

"Where are you?" Fancy asked.

"In the streets, taking care of business," he replied coolly.

"Well, your business needs to be with me, Nasir. We need to meet, and soon," she said pointedly.

"We will, Fancy. Why the fuck you trippin'?"

"Nasir, why do I feel like you've been avoiding me since I had that meeting with Jesus? Are you jealous of my position?" Fancy asked.

Nasir was revolted by the question. "Hell nah!" he spat.

"Then good, cuz our first shipment is supposed to arrive soon and we can't fuck this up. I need you by my side, baby," Fancy said.

"And I'm here, ready to get this money," he said halfheartedly.

"Okay, as long as we have that understanding," Fancy replied sternly, making it clear that she was the boss.

Their call ended, and Nasir was left with a grimace across his face. He pulled out a cigarette, lit it quickly, and started the ignition to his car. He took a few strong pulls from the Newport and exhaled. Fancy had rubbed him the wrong way. He saw things changing between them, but he kept cool about it. With the cartel backing her, there was nothing he could do at the moment but follow instructions. The young girl was fully dressed and ready to be dropped off. She was no longer a concern to him; she had satisfied him completely and he didn't have any more use for her.

Nasir pulled off the block and decided to take her home to Bushwick, Brooklyn. The ride was silent. Nasir's mind was spinning with so many things. The only thing he wanted to do right now was get something to eat, check on his niggas on the block, and get high.

He pulled up to the dilapidated row houses on the shabby Brooklyn block, and his female companion stepped out of his ride, pulling down her short skirt.

She closed the door, but before she went inside, she went back to the passenger window, rested her elbows against the door frame and said to Nasir, "You know I'm here for you whenever you want . . . especially if you want some of this pussy. I got you, Nasir, remember that."

Nasir remained deadpan. He would take her up on her offer soon, but not tonight. Tonight he had things to take care of and people he wanted to talk to. Before the little tramp could enter her home, Nasir was already down block and making a right turn. He got on his phone and called his mother. She answered after the fourth ring.

"Nasir, what you want?" Brenda asked roughly.

Nasir knew he had treated his mother wrong in the past months, but somehow, he needed her guidance—some motherly advice from her, even though the truth had come out that she wasn't really his biological mother. She was the only mother he knew and there was no one else.

"You home?" he asked.

"Yes, Nasir."

"I need to talk to you."

"When?"

"Tonight," he said. "A couple hours."

"Okay, see you then."

He hung up. It was still early in the evening and he made a few other phone calls, mostly to his new crew to check up on things in the streets. After Nasir's homies—Shoe-Shine, Nicholas and Lucky—were murdered, he had to fan out and recruit some thoroughbreds to keep his organization flourishing.

Nasir pulled up in front of his mother's building toking on a phat, burning blunt. He lingered behind the wheel of his Benz for a moment, listening to Meek Mills' *Dreams and Nightmares* album and trying to get his thoughts together. The .45 was visible in the passenger seat. The block was quiet on a chilly March night. He didn't see any of his peoples around, and found it strange.

Nasir finished off the blunt and dowsed the remnants into the ashtray. He then picked up the pistol and stuffed it into his waistband, concealing the weapon with his shirt and jacket. He stepped out of his car with his head held high and confidence. This was his block and his hood, and he always felt at home in Brooklyn.

He strutted into his mother's building and took the stairs up.

After four loud knocks, Brenda snatched open the door with a scowl and spat, "Damn-it, Nasir, what you knocking so got-damn hard on my fuckin' door for?"

"I missed you too, Ma, but you knew I was coming by," he said, pushing by her and barging into her apartment without an invite.

"I ain't think this fuckin' soon, nigga!" she cursed. "You said in a couple hours."

"Well I'm here now."

Brenda closed the door, and then closed and tied her robe together to cover her nudity. She then threw her hands on her hips and shifted her weight onto one leg. She fixed her eyes on her son, who looked like a don thug in all his name-brand attire, brand new Timberlands, and gleaming jewelry.

"You look good, Nasir," she said.

Nasir didn't respond to his mother's compliment. He briefly looked around the apartment. She was living like ghetto royalty, thanks to Fancy. The once run-down decor had done a 180 with flat-screen televisions, leather furniture, and a lavish dining-room set, along with a high-end stereo system with the latest DVDs and CDs scattered everywhere.

"I need to talk," he said to his mother in low tone.

Brenda was ready to listen. But something else seemed to be on her mind. She lashed out at Nasir by saying, "Nigga, you should have given me a specific time that you was comin' by. You can't just be comin' the fuck by at any got-damn hour!"

"Why not?" he replied with sarcasm. "And I coulda used my key."

"Muthafucka, cuz I got fuckin' company in the bedroom," she exclaimed.

Nasir glanced at the black Timberland boots in the corner and the black leather jacket draped over one of the dining room chairs.

"Tell that nigga to leave before I tell him. I got sumthin' important to discuss wit' you, and I don't need any other prying ears around," he said roughly.

Brenda felt that her son wasn't going to come into her home and dictate what she needed to do. She had been in the middle of a great fuck with her legs spread wide, her ass arched in the air and her face buried into the pillow, taking the nine-inch dick like a pro until Nasir came knocking loudly.

"I was in the middle of sumthin' good, Nasir."

"Either you tell the nigga to leave politely your way, or I tell the nigga to leave my way." He lifted up his shirt to reveal the gun in his waistband, indicating to Brenda that things could get ugly.

Brenda scowled heavily. "You think you still live here and fuckin' run things?"

Nasir didn't have time to argue with his mother. He pivoted in the direction of the bedroom and started to march down the narrow hallway.

"Nasir, please, just give me some fuckin' respect! I'll tell him to leave," Brenda uttered. "Okay!"

She frowned, cursed some more, and walked by her son to reluctantly do the task herself, but before she could make it to the bedroom, her young, male company came charging out of the back bedroom halfway dressed with a .9mm gripped in his hand. Nasir recognized the man immediately. It was one of his young lieutenants from the streets.

Nasir was shocked to see the man, especially having sexual relations with his mother. He heard him say, "Nasir, I ain't know she was ya moms, yo! I swear to it!" He had panic written across his face.

With the .9mm aimed at Nasir, it seemed like all hell was about to break loose.

"Li'l-Un, you need to really chill out, put the gun down, and get the fuck out," Nasir told him calmly. He didn't have time to reach for his own weapon, so he had to think.

Li'l-Un was shaky and nervous. "Yo, I ain't know she was ya moms, yo. She came on to me and initiated this shit," he explained wildly.

Brenda didn't want any bloodshed in her apartment but if somebody had to die, it wasn't gonna be Nasir. She glared at her young lover, and shouted, "Are you fuckin' crazy?"

Nasir had a bone to pick with both of them. He already had a lot on his mind, and now he had to see this shit. Li'l-Un had the upper hand for now. He had the gun. He looked nervous and unpredictable. Nasir didn't want to die tonight or any night in the near future. He began to walk backwards into the living room with his hands in the air indicating his temporary surrender.

"You got this, Li'l-Un . . . it's all good. Just be on ya way, nigga, a'ight? It's all good, just go, and I'm gonna forget this incident ever happened," Nasir said in a cool manner.

Li'l-Un's eyes were wild with fear and survival.

"You swear? You ain't lying, right?" Li'l-Un replied.

Nasir glared at him and replied. "I swear."

He knew about Nasir's violent temper. He was leaving the apartment alive by any means necessary. He held the gun at Nasir and his moms and kept saying, "The bitch came at me, yo, the bitch came at me. But I know you strapped, nigga . . . drop that shit slowly on the floor."

"Are you crazy!" Brenda hollered. "Just fuckin' leave, you stupid muthafucka!"

"Ma, shut the fuck up!" Nasir shouted.

Reluctantly, Nasir did what he was told. He slowly removed the pistol from his waistband, placed it on the floor, and kicked it over to Li'l-Un's direction. Li'l-Un picked it up and stuffed the gun into his waistband. He now had full control of the room.

Nasir glared at his lieutenant. He wanted to tear him apart. Li'l-Un carefully gathered his things in the room and then put on his Timbs with the gun trained at Nasir. He moved near the door and said to them, "Yo, I'm sorry, Nasir, I ain't know. I didn't want it to be like this, fo' real. I'm sorry, man."

"Yeah, you sorry, just get the fuck out, and don't let me see you ever again in Brooklyn or wherever," Nasir replied through clenched teeth.

Li'l-Un rushed out the door and sprinted down the hallway, leaping down the stairway toward the exit with his heart racing vigorously. He had pulled out a pistol on his boss and not used it and also fucked his boss's moms—he knew it was a fatal mistake.

Nasir was so furious, that when Li'l-Un left, he turned and threw his fist into the wall, creating a gaping hole in the weak sheetrock. He shouted, "I'ma kill that nigga!"

Brenda was dumbfounded for a moment. Her night was ruined. Nasir shot a cold look at his moms and charged at her. Brenda became terrified. She stumbled back and almost tripped over a chair in the room. Nasir grabbed his moms with brute force by her robe and was tempted to strike her, but he didn't. The look in his eyes was contemptuous. He came to have a serious talk with her and had to stumble into some bullshit.

"What, you gonna hit your own mother now?" she dared him.

Nasir released her and stepped away. He just needed to think about things.

"Where are the kids?" he asked.

"Over at my friend's house for the night," she said.

Nasir went into one of the other bedrooms to be alone for a minute. He wanted to talk to his mother, but not at the moment. He needed to calm down before he killed her.

"Nasir, I thought you wanted to talk . . . Nasir," Brenda called out.

Nasir disappeared into the bedroom and slammed the door behind him, drowning out his mother's calling. Brenda knew better than to interrupt or push her son over the edge, so she decided to give him some space.

Nasir took a few strong pulls from the purple haze burning between his lips and stared out the window for a moment. Dawn was approaching soon and the block was quiet. The apartment was calm also, his little brothers and sister were still at a friend's house. Nasir still had the incident with Li'l-Un on his mind and decided he would deal with it later. He wanted that nigga's head on a spike. But at the moment, he had other things to worry about.

He exhaled the smoke and sat back on the couch. Brenda walked into the living room. She gazed at her son and lit a cigarette of her own to smoke. Nasir cut his eyes at his mother and remained quiet for a short moment. Li'l-Un was nineteen and she had the audacity not only to rob the cradle, but to fuck one of his lieutenants.

Brenda gazed at her son and asked, "Are you still upset with me?"

"Out of everybody in Brooklyn, you had to fuck wit' him," said Nasir.

"I'm a grown woman, Nasir, and he's over the age," she said, justifying her actions. "I just needed some dick, and he was around to give it to me."

Nasir took another pull from the blunt and shook his head. Brenda moved closer to her son. She continued smoking and was more decent in a pair of sweat pants and a long T-shirt. She fixed her eyes on Nasir and knew there was something else troubling him.

"How are you and Fancy doing?" she asked.

Nasir remained silent. Brenda took a seat on the couch near her son. For a moment, each was lost in their own thoughts. Nasir continued to smoke weed and Brenda lit another cigarette and inhaled the strong nicotine.

Nasir turned to his mother and said, "We wit' a cartel now."

"What?" Brenda looked confused.

"Several days ago, Fancy and I, or I'll just say Fancy met wit' Jesus, one of most dangerous figures in the underworld. He's in control of everything, Ma . . . runs his cartel wit' an iron fist, and he put Fancy in charge of everything," Nasir proclaimed.

Brenda was shocked. Fancy had definitely come a long way, from being the pretentious little bitch that first showed up at her apartment door looking for a place to stay to the queen-pin of the streets. Brenda was happy to finally be on her good side.

Nasir continued talking. He told her how he felt about the situation. He didn't like it. He didn't understand why the cartel would put so much faith in Fancy and he was starting to distrust her. She had too much power—too much for a female. And even though they were in a relationship, and supposedly in love, why would she still need him around? Nasir felt like he'd helped create a monster.

Brenda explained to him that it was all her sister's Belen's fault.

"What you mean?" Nasir inquired.

"Fancy wants her mother home, right? She's the only parent around, and believe me, Belen can be a very devious and manipulative bitch, even to her own daughter. Y'all could be working to free Belen out of prison for the rest of y'all young lives. Why else would Jesus give Fancy so much power? The two are probably in cahoots with each other."

Nasir remained quiet.

"Nasir, you gonna have to think smart and don't rush into things. This is chess, not checkers. You were put into a very prominent position, so you make the best of it. You continue to play your position with the cartel and protect Fancy. She's your love, and she's family. And look at the positive side with linking up with the cartel—the power you have and knowing nobody won't dare fuck with you in the game. And you have the chance to expand your own organization out there. Even though you have to answer to them, you still run your own crew and have these streets on lockdown," Brenda proclaimed. "You are a don, son."

Nasir nodded.

Brenda saw the power and prosperity that would come with Fancy and her son doing business with such a large drug cartel, and she also wanted to reap the benefits from it. It was somewhat a proud day for her.

Her son Nasir had come up in a major way and she yearned to be the mother of a major kingpin. She wanted to move out of Brooklyn and into an extravagant mansion somewhere in Long Island, and have access to unlimited wealth. Yes, she wanted the lifestyle her sister Belen had.

Nasir continued to smoke his weed and took in everything his mother was telling him. "You right, Ma," he said coolly. "You right."

"I know I'm right, baby. You know how many of these niggas out here would love to be in your position? This is a golden opportunity for you, baby—for us. Let Fancy hold the reigns to the iron throne, but you stay right behind her commanding the army. They respect you out here, Nasir, and you let it be fuckin' known what you about."

Nasir wanted to be a legend in the streets. Brooklyn was his playground, but he wanted to make New York his kingdom.

They continued to talk until dawn surfaced and the sunlight began percolating through the living room window. They started to come up with a game plan to try and keep one step ahead of everyone else, because working with the cartel was profitable, but also risky—and the last thing Brenda wanted to see, was her son murdered and then butchered like some cow.

"You be smart and cautious about everything, Nasir . . . you and Fancy. You hear me, son?"

"I'm always smart about things, Ma," he replied with assurance.

Brenda gazed at her son and noticed the change in him. She remembered not too long ago when he was just a young, punk hustler on the block, using her kitchen to cook up crack. Now he was a heavyweight with a direct contact to a cartel. Everything was changing in their world, and Brenda hoped it continued to change for the better.

She retreated back into her bedroom while Nasir went to sleep on the couch. It had been a really busy day for him, and he needed his rest.

KIM K.

Several hours later, Nasir stepped out of his mother's building after getting some much-needed rest. It was early afternoon and a little chilly in the Brooklyn air. Nasir jumped into his Benz, lit a cigarette, and drove away. He decided to go home to see Fancy and have few words with her, but before that, he had to handle a situation on the streets. He drove around Brooklyn in search of Li'l-Un. He didn't forget that the nigga pulled a gun on him and fucked his mother. The nigga had to die for the ultimate disrespect.

Nasir came to a stop in front of a local and dilapidated corner bodega where a few of his goons were lingering outside. The men on the corner recognized the car with the blaring rap music immediately. The passenger window came rolling down and Nasir leaned forward, staring at his goons and hollered out, "Pete, Jo-Jo, let me holla at y'all niggas fo' a minute."

The two young hoodlums didn't need to ask questions; it was their boss calling, so they walked over to the gleaming Benz with their sagging jeans and winter attire and waited to hear what he had to say to them.

"Ay, y'all seen Li'l-Un around today?" Nasir asked.

"Nah, Nasir, we ain't seen the nigga on the block," said Pete.

"Yo, if y'all niggas do, holla at me ASAP. I need to holla at the nigga about sumthin' important," Nasir told them. "Keep it on the low."

They nodded.

"We got you, boss," Jo-Jo replied.

Nasir put a C-note in each man's hand to get the word out that he was looking for Li'l-Un. Pete and Jo-Jo were truly excited and appreciated the extra cash in their hand. Nasir rolled his window back up and drove off. Li'l-Un was going to turn up sooner or later. He was confident about that.

CHAPTER SIX

Nasir pulled up to the stylish three-bedroom condo in the suburbs of north Bergen County New Jersey. It was located at the northeastern corner of the state, bordered by Rockland County, New York to the north, and by Manhattan and the Bronx across the Hudson river to the east. The area was blanketed with trees and rolling hills, with a beautiful view of miles of the countryside. It was miles away from his Brooklyn stomping grounds and different—peaceful. North New Jersey was where the privileged lived—the doctors, lawyers, surgeons, and businessmen and women that had that large piece of the American dream and more.

The condo was an investment property that Nasir and Fancy planned to hold just long enough to sell and make a profit. In the meantime, they enjoyed it from time to time. New Jersey was far away, but still close enough to home. The over-the-top condo was only the beginning for them, though. With the money they expected to bring in from dealing with the cartel, she expected to see herself living it up in sprawling mansions, going on hundred thousand-dollar shopping sprees and having her own fleet of luxury vintage cars. And she didn't see herself making the same mistakes as her parents. She was smarter than that. She would be a lot more careful and keep her circle tight, and would establish a legitimate business to launder her drug money.

The last thing Fancy wanted to see was incarceration.

Nasir exited his car and walked toward the sprawling complex with his hand close to his burner. He may have been out of the hood, but the hood wasn't out of him, and sometimes he could be a bit paranoid. Even though he was surrounded by well-established upper and middle-class people who didn't have an ounce of streets in them, he didn't trust anyone—rich or poor. Nasir didn't give a fuck.

He used his key to enter the condo. It was well furnished with the cream of the crop of everything. The place was dimly lit and silent. Nasir moved through the condo looking for Fancy. He gripped his pistol in his hand and slowly made his way toward the back room when he noticed the light on in the bathroom. The door was ajar, and when he gazed inside, he exhaled a little when he saw Fancy soaking peacefully in the sunken oval tub enjoying a soothing bubble bath.

He made his way inside the sweet-smelling bathroom with the scented candles burning, illuminating the bathroom in a dreamy hue.

Nasir eyed his lady for a moment, taking in all of her beauty. She had her eyes closed, listening to the soothing and sensual sound of Sade.

Fancy's womanly curves were so enticing and alluring that the more he stared, the harder his erection grew in his jeans. He walked toward the tub and startled Fancy with his sudden presence. She jumped and caused a ripple through the waters.

"Shit, Nasir, you scared the shit out of me!" she exclaimed.

"You should be a little more cautious, Fancy. I know we ain't in the hood anymore, but always keep ya gun close," he warned her.

"I will."

Fancy removed herself from the tub, her naked body glistening with remnants of the soapy water. She reached for her towel and started to towel off in front of Nasir. He stood close by and watched, enjoying the small show she inadvertently put on. They hadn't had sex in two weeks, and he had the urge to pull her into his arms and ravage her body from head to toe. Her body was so amazing that she could effortlessly hypnotize any man with her nakedness.

Fancy noticed Nasir's lingering gaze on her body and uttered, "You find anything interesting?"

He found a lot of things interesting. And it wasn't only sex. He wanted to talk to Fancy. First, he wanted to know if a hunk of their money was going to help with Belen's release. He understood she cared about her mother, but their finances couldn't be tied up in attorney fees, commissary, and appeals. Second, he wanted to know when they were going to meet with Jesus' right-hand man, Amarillo. He operated the south coast of Miami shorelines and oversaw the boats of freight that controlled everything arriving in the country from Colombia to Miami.

Nasir was ready to get his hands on such quantity of product and put the work out on the streets, knowing anything coming from Jesus' cartel would be very potent. His crew was out there, ready to become significant distributors in the game.

"Any word on the shipment yet? I got my niggas hungry out there for some work," he asked. He felt everything was at a standstill for a moment.

Fancy knotted her towel to keep it from falling and replied, "You can't rush things with these men, Nasir. They do things their way and at their own pace. This is a very large shipment—damn near five hundred or more kilos coming into our grasps, and I would hate to think what would happen if we fucked it up."

"We not gonna fuck this shit up, Fancy. Don't even think like that. We were bred to do this shit, you hear me?" said Nasir halfheartedly.

He truly believed that he was bred to do this, but not her. But he didn't want to discourage Fancy when such a large shipment was about to arrive. Everybody had to be on their A game.

Fancy nodded.

She went over to the large bathroom mirror and paid attention to her reflection for a moment. She dealt with her hair and was trying to get ready for the evening. Nasir stood behind her and gazed at his own image. He continued talking to Fancy, asking, "What's goin' on wit' ya mom's appeal? When was the last time you went to visit her? And I hope a large chunk of our finances isn't goin' to lawyers and whatnot. She lived her life, Fancy; now it's time to live ours."

Fancy turned around to glare at Nasir and spat, "What's goin' on with my mother is my business, not yours, Nasir. And I'm handling things. Don't worry about it. We about to get this large shipment from the Colombians and when it comes, you need to focus only on that."

"And I will," he replied. "But you are my concern too."

"I appreciate your care, but I can handle my own."

"I know you can. I don't doubt that."

"You shouldn't!"

Fancy turned back to the mirror and moved a comb through her long, sensuous hair. She then stared at Nasir through the mirror and asked, "Do you have a problem with me being in charge of things, Nasir?"

Nasir was straight-laced. He replied with, "Nah, no problem." It was a feeble reply.

"You sure? Because ever since that meeting with Jesus, I felt things have changed somewhat between you and me. You've become a little aloof toward me."

"I just want us to be careful, baby. These Colombians I just don't trust like that."

"And we will be, baby."

Nasir wasn't the one to sugarcoat anything, and he abruptly asked, "But why you, Fancy?"

"What you mean?"

"Did you ever think or ask yourself why a man like Jesus would put a woman he doesn't even know into such a powerful position? I mean, no offense Fancy, but what makes you so special? I mean, I brought you into the game and taught you about the streets. You've sold drugs, but you ain't no drug dealer."

Fancy was ready to scream out that he was her father, but she held her tongue and kept her composure.

"It's because he has respect for my parents. He knows what kind of people I come from," she said and rolled her eyes.

Nasir thought it was bullshit. There was something more going on, and he didn't fully trust the situation. But they had already made a deal with the devil and their signature was signed in blood. There was no backing out now and he had no choice but to run with it. Everyone's lives were on the line.

"Your father was a powerful man, but this muthafucka . . . he makes me tense."

Fancy locked eyes with Nasir, and she noticed something different inside of him. Her man wasn't any punk. He was a killer just like the rest of them, but the look in his eyes showed great concern . . . or was it jealousy? Did he suddenly have doubts now because he wasn't the one pulling the strings?

"Nasir, I'm smart and I can handle Jesus or anybody else. You forget who my father was, and my mother," Fancy proclaimed with attitude.

"But you're neither one of them. It wasn't long ago when you ain't know shit about drugs or murder. Now you think you're a professional at this."

Fancy spun around with her face distorted from anger. "So what you trying to say, Nasir? That I'm stupid and can't lead? Fuck you! I'm the head bitch in charge of all of this. I came this far and I refuse to fall. Haven't I proven myself enough to you and everybody that doubted me? I fuckin' built this—"

"No, I fuckin' built this and you rode shotgun!" he chided back. "I was the one with the coke and heroin. It was my soldiers out there bussing their guns and expanding our clientele. I was the one protecting you and took a fuckin' bullet for you! I was the one that had ya back in these streets! I taught you everything you know—"

"Yes you did, but I perfected the hustle," she retorted. "I was the chosen one!"

That statement angered Nasir. She didn't perfect shit. It was only a series of fortunate events that propelled her into an esteemed position, and now things were going to her head.

"You the boss, baby," Nasir replied, mockingly.

"Damn right I am, and don't you forget it." Fancy returned. "Baby."

Nasir was ready to leave the bathroom. Fancy's cell phone ringing on the marble countertop paused his exit. Fancy stared at the caller I.D.; it was a New Jersey number that she didn't recognize at all. She answered and immediately the voice on the other end was demanding and raspy.

"Negro says hello," the man said.

"Who is this?"

"Amarillo," he announced heavily.

It was the phone call Fancy had been waiting for. She perked up and almost found herself speechless. She gazed at Nasir with a "this is it" look and walked closer to her man. He wanted to hear the conversation too.

Amarillo continued with, "First, do not put me on speaker phone. My instructions are for your ears only . . . comprende?"

Fancy's eyes widened. It seemed like he'd just read her mind.

"Yes," she replied softly.

"Dos . . . now tomorrow night is the delivery. You do as we say, and everything will go smoothly. As you know, we don't like problems, so do not create any problems. Comprende?"

"I understand."

"Now, I will call back tomorrow afternoon around three with further instructions. You pick up, don't speak, and come to the address given to you. You remember the address and don't write anything down. Comprende?"

"Yes."

"Tomorrow, phone call at three sharp. No jodas con esto!" he stated.

Fancy understood some of what he said, meaning she must not fuck up.

The call ended and Fancy found herself nervous and eager at the same time. Nasir wanted to know what the man said.

"It was him, Amarillo, and he said he'll call back tomorrow afternoon with the location," she said.

This was it.

It was a brisk evening in New Jersey. One final snowfall was predicted to start tomorrow, until the days of spring came.

Fancy steered her gleaming BMW through the streets of Jersey City and toward the industrial area near the Hudson River. Nasir was with her, anticipating meeting the connect. The ride to finally meet with Amarillo at an abandoned warehouse was a very tense one. They were instructed to come alone and they did. It wasn't a negotiation, and they didn't make the rules, but could only follow them. The sun was slowly fading behind the horizon, bringing dusk over the city. The Jersey City streets were gradually becoming sparse with traffic.

Fancy maneuvered through the streets and to the sprawling large warehouse that sat nestled in the back streets of Jersey City. When they reached the gates, two husky Colombian armed men were outside waiting for her arrival. Fancy slowly drove up to the structure and stepped out onto the gravel pavement in her stiletto heels and tight jeans that highlighted her thick curves and a butter-soft leather jacket. She looked more like a young model with her angelic features and curvy shape than a rising drug queen-pin.

One of the Colombian henchmen got on a two-way radio and called out to his boss. He spoke Spanish, informing his boss that their company had arrived.

"Dejarlos en el interior," the voice through the two-way radio instructed.

The guard nodded.

Before they made any further movement, they were both checked for any weapons, and the men thoroughly looked through the car too. It was all cleared.

"Inside," the guard said to Fancy and Nasir.

The steel gate lifted, and Fancy drove her BMW into the warehouse, where dozens of empty pallets were spread everywhere. She immediately noticed several men carefully and skillfully taking apart two eighteen-wheeler tractor-trailers in the middle of the warehouse. It didn't take a rocket scientist to know what was going on and how the drugs were shipped to New York.

Several dark SUVs were parked around, and numerous armed men clutching machine guns and semi-automatics stood about. Security in the warehouse was tighter than Ft. Knox. Fancy kept cool, even though she felt like a sheep in a lions' den. She kept a pokerfaced expression and waited to see the man in charge.

There was a man smoking a Cuban cigar seated by a long table that was cluttered with a few laptops, some paperwork, and guns. He was speaking Spanish to the men that surrounded him. He had full control of the room, and his demeanor displayed that he was the boss man. He stood about five-six with his muscular build, and had no facial hair and a gleaming bald head. He was dressed to the nines in a black tailored suit and wingtip shoes. Fancy assumed it had to be Amarillo.

He stood from his chair, looked over at Nasir and Fancy, and waved them over, shouting out, "Come here!"

Flanked by Nasir, she walked over to the table. Amarillo took a few pulls from his cigar and sized up the lovely looking, gangster-ass couple. Nasir kept a stone face and his fists clenched. He hated being helpless and defenseless. He had to keep cool, but it was hard protecting Fancy when he was one man against an army.

"Rojo, I assume," said Amarillo with a smile.

"I am," she said.

"You are younger than I expected," he said.

"Age is only a number, but taking care of business is a mindset," she replied.

"This is a man's business, I feel, but if Negro wants a young girl to run things up here, then it's his call . . . perra joven necesita su pop cherry, hey." Amarillo turned to his men and said.

They laughed, staring at Fancy.

Fancy knew they were all laughing at her expense. She vaguely understood his Spanish, hearing the words bitch and cherry in the same sentence. But she couldn't do anything about the disrespect. She was there for business, not to make friends.

"You ready for this? This is a huge load to distribute, and I would hate to imagine what would happen if you fuck it up," said Amarillo.

"She is!" Nasir stepped forward and spoke.

Amarillo eyed the young thug.

"And you are?"

"I'm her man, and I have her back every step of the way," Nasir replied firmly.

Amarillo took a pull from his cigar. His stout presence was intimidating, but Nasir didn't show any sign of weakness. He was from the mean Brooklyn streets, and if men like Amarillo stepped foot on his turf with any sign of disrespect, then they would immediately be gunned down.

"I admire your courage," said Amarillo. He then turned to his goons and uttered with heartiness, "Que podria ser una oveja jugando lobo, aunque . . ."

The men laughed again.

Nasir wished he understood what they were saying. But it didn't take knowing the language to know that he was being clowned. Nasir frowned. He didn't like that muthafucka.

In the background, numerous drills and heavy machinery were taking apart the large trucks. It was becoming noisy and harder to hear anyone speak. The Colombians were skilled at concealment, using hidden compartments in tractor-trailers to transport tons of drugs across the country.

"It is noisy in here, hey . . . we talk somewhere else," Amarillo said to his guests.

Fancy nodded.

Amarillo gestured to an empty back office. He led the way, and Nasir and Fancy followed behind him. They entered the dusty and dirty office. The entire place seemed abandoned for years. Amarillo flicked on the lights and took a seat in a folding chair. He didn't care about his suit; he owned thousands worth thousands.

"It will be a while before we extract the product from the truck. My men are fast at work and you will have your product soon," he said calmly.

The noise of the workers was still heard, but was to some extent drowned out by the office walls. Nasir turned and watched the men work through the dirty and tarnished window. There were over two dozen men tearing apart everything, from the two custom-built canisters mounted on the outside of the trailer, to the air filters, air compressors, exhaust stacks, tubeless tires, fuel tanks, battery boxes, hydraulic systems, underneath the cab, the sleeper compartment, tractor doors, cab storage doors, and other miscellaneous hidden places.

It seemed like lions devouring their prey in the wilderness. Slowly, but surely, tons and tons of cocaine and heroin were being removed from everywhere in the truck. It was a wonder to watch.

"Are you impressed?" Amarillo asked Nasir.

Nasir turned and looked at him. He nonchalantly replied, "Over coke? Not at all."

Amarillo smirked. He continued smoking his cigar.

"I was informed that your arrangement with Negro is that you will leave here with five hundred kilos," he added.

"It is," Fancy replied.

"Sometimes the boss can get overzealous with things," he said pointedly and chuckled.

It was obvious in Amarillo's eyes that he was against it. But Jesus was the boss and he had to trust his judgment. He gazed at Fancy for a moment, making her feel a little bit uneasy. Nasir noticed the steely glare and pompous tone toward Fancy, and he didn't like it one bit. He was ready to step in and say something offensive. He didn't care where he was at and who was who. Fancy was the woman he loved.

"He's the boss, and it's the reason why he's where he is and you are where you are," Fancy replied complacently.

The look on Amarillo's face showed that he wasn't too pleased with Fancy's remark. She beamed on the inside and so did Nasir.

"You are a bold little one," replied Amarillo.

"I'm ambitious; always gonna get what I want, by any means necessary, just like Belen Lane. I'm sure you heard of her," Fancy proclaimed.

"I have, even met her. She was ruthless. But isn't she dead now? Or something close to it? Those that don't know how to stay in their lane get run over as soon as the race starts."

"Well, I've been in the race for a long time, and I'm running in my lane just fine," she quipped.

"It's a long race, and some people don't even cross the finish line . . . puede ser un juego peligroso," replied Amarillo.

Fancy smiled. It was somewhat entertaining for her to go tit-for-tat with Amarillo. Like everyone else, he doubted her, but she was ready to prove what type of woman he was dealing with.

Several hours went by until both tractor-trailers were dismantled and over 1,500 kilos were removed from the hidden compartments. There was a gold mine of white powder stacked up on pallets. The men were exhausted and sweaty.

"Damn!" Fancy uttered.

She was ready to take her share and leave.

Subtly, Fancy's five hundred kilos were concealed into a false bottom of a long, U-Haul van by the men and ready to depart. Their lives were on the line. This was it. Nasir would be the driver. He was handed the keys. He climbed inside and started the ignition. Everything was on point and legit, and they were ready to go.

Amarillo gazed at Fancy. He had a new cigar lit and burning between his fingers. He took a pull from it and exhaled. He said to Fancy with his smug stare, "Welcome to the big leagues. I just hope you make the cut . . . or porque si no lo hace, a continuacion, le cortamos."

The men laughed again.

Fancy wasn't worried. She strutted to her parked BMW, climbed inside, and started the ignition. Her engine roared like a tiger. She revved the engine and stared at Amarillo. "Like Arnold in the Terminator . . . 'I'll be back.'"

She laughed at her own one-liner and followed behind Nasir in the U-Haul van.

They drove into New York and to a safe location in Brooklyn. They wasted no time putting a tight and trusted crew together to process some of the kilos for the streets and trafficking a majority of the drugs across state lines. At eighteen thousand dollars a ki, with over four hundred kilos to ship out, they were looking to make an estimate of an eight– to nine-million-dollar profit from this heavy batch alone.

Fancy had succeeded in becoming the successor to her parents'—or her mother's—drug organization. She was seated on the throne and felt proud to be at the top. To those who had doubted her, she was ready to scream, "Look at me now, bitches!"

CHAPTER 7

Fancy sat at the small, crèche-looking table with her legs crossed, surrounded by dozens of female inmates and their visitors in the harsh concrete environment, and waited for her mother reluctantly. She was dressed like a diva in her Donna Karan attire with her hair and makeup flawlessly done. This was the last place she wanted to be on one of the few nicest days in March. Finally, the weather was breaking, reaching sixty degrees, and spring was right around the corner. And Fancy wanted to throw the top back on her sky-blue BMW and cruise around New York stunting.

She was a busy woman now with over five hundred kilos to distribute from New York to South Carolina. The lost little girl with nowhere to go after her mother's incarceration didn't even seem to exist. The transition was fast and brutal for her. And she had a point to prove to everyone—failure was not an option.

It was only because of Nasir's urging that Fancy took the time out from her new lifestyle to come visit her mother. She had done enough for her mother, and her mother had done enough for her. The attorney fees for filing her appeal and criminal case were adding up, and Fancy felt Belen was only using her. Nasir felt they should cut all ties with her. It was too risky to keep visiting, especially with their newfound position with the drug cartel. He felt having ties to Belen would trigger a federal investigation on themselves. So he also urged Fancy to visit her mother and let it be known that this would be their last visit.

Fancy yearned for a cigarette as she sat and waited. The female inmates started to pile into the large visiting room, and Fancy spotted her mother immediately in the middle of the line. Belen looked around for her daughter; this time she sat closer to the inmates' entrance.

Times had changed, and feelings too. The usual hugs, smiles and kisses exchanged between mother and daughter no longer existed. Instead, the two treated each other like business associates, or like estranged friends. Belen's features seemed to become more hardened with her long cornrows and the hard lines forming in her face. She was looking older and stressed out about so many things. She would be soon transferred to the federal prison in Hazelton, West Virginia. She had less than six months.

"Hey Mom," Fancy greeted dryly.

Belen sighed heavily and gazed at her daughter who once again was looking amazing in her pristine attire with her natural, long hair flowing down to her butt.

"Always looking like a diva to come see me, huh? You trying to make some kind of statement toward me, Fancy?" Belen asked with some bite in her tone.

Fancy chuckled lightly. She was aware of her mother's jealous antics and sardonic remarks.

"I just like to look nice, Mother. You know I always do. You raised me and watched me grow up; it's in my blood," she replied with a faint smile.

Fancy couldn't say the same about her mother's image. She had been aging more and more every day, and always looking like a dyke. Fancy wondered if her mother took to eating pussy and being sodomized by broomsticks and other foreign objects while on the inside. She damn sure didn't have access to any dick unless one of the male guards was fucking her. Belen still had a very nice shape and luscious breasts that sat on her chest naturally without any support. And Fancy knew her mother was definitely eye candy for every gay bitch inside.

"How you holding up?" asked Fancy.

"I could be better," she replied faintly. "But you, Fancy, you are a disrespectful little bitch!" Her mother accosted underneath her breath.

"And why am I a bitch, Mother?"

"My attorney fees haven't been taken care of yet, and me applying for this appeal is quickly approaching. I need you to handle this. I need to be home soon."

Fancy thought her mother was delusional. Freedom for her wasn't going to happen anytime soon—very likely not at all. Belen's name had been torn apart by the newspapers and the media—her true identity revealed. They said Belen was responsible for dozens of murders during her reign as a drug queen-pin. She made millions of dollars and was on her way to becoming one of the most untouchable bitches in the game. Her rags to riches story and criminal case even reached the White House and had the president's attention. Rappers acknowledged Belen in their rhymes, and publishers were approaching her to write a tell-all book. Even *Vibe* and *Feds* magazine wanted to do an article on her.

Belen wasn't a snitch, and she wasn't telling her story to anyone, no matter how much money they offered her. A tell-all book would put her life on the line with the cartel and so many others.

The fame and notoriety Belen had made for herself made Nasir extremely nervous. But Fancy didn't even break a sweat about it.

"I'm still working on it, Mom. Five hundred thousand dollars to drop on one lawyer is a lot of damn money," said Fancy.

"For my freedom, it's worth it, Fancy. And when was the last time you reached out to Gary Scheck to see what's going on with my appeal?"

"He's a very busy man."

"You make got-damn time to go and see this lawyer and make sure he handles my appeal correctly. I can't fuck this up. He needs his money and he needs to visit me," Belen said strongly.

Fancy listened.

"Don't fuck me over on this, Fancy. I don't care how big you get in these streets; I'm still your fucking mother. I'm the bitch that everyone is talking about, and I'm the bitch that connected you with Jesus. I was the one that breathed life into you," Belen proclaimed profoundly.

She clenched her fists and added, "So don't ever take me for granted, little girl."

"I thank you for everything you did for me. But I'm a different woman now. I am a better woman. And my newfound position in Jesus' cartel, moving four to five hundred kilos a week, will solidify me into dominance over everything. I am you, Mommy, but only better," Fancy said with a pretentious tone.

"Are you fucking crazy, Fancy?" Belen hollered out.

Her loud outburst startled those around her and made the guards shoot a steely glare at her. They rose up and were ready to leap into action, but Belen quickly composed herself and glared at her daughter.

"Why?" Belen asked.

"Because he sees so much potential in me," was Fancy's reply.

Belen was shocked but also worried. She felt Fancy wasn't ready for such a large task. She didn't understand why a man like Jesus, in his position, with thousands of employees and loyal lieutenants, would give an inexperienced young female so much responsibility. It didn't add up, and there was no way Fancy would be able to move that much weight, especially on a weekly basis. Shit, in her prime in the game, she and her husband weren't moving that much weight in a week, maybe even a month.

Belen was expecting Jesus to make it easier on her daughter and probably have her move a couple of kilos a week. She couldn't figure out his angle. She didn't trust the arrangement.

"Fancy, don't be so damn naive. I don't trust this," she clearly let it be known.

"You don't have to trust it, but I do. I know what I'm doing," Fancy said with conviction. "And no matter what you say or believe, we already received the first shipment several days ago and everything went out as planned," she said in a low voice, for only her mother to hear.

"This isn't fucking Brooklyn you're dealing with. These men aren't young corner thugs dealing with a kilo here or there and carrying a pistol in their jeans. This is a violent, murderous, and well-organized cartel that will slaughter any man and woman, even child, in a heartbeat if shit goes wrong, Fancy."

"So far I'm doing okay with them, Mother," Fancy replied. "People underestimated me, and look at me now."

Belen couldn't get her point across through her daughter's thick and ignorant head. Fancy saw the money and the power, but Belen was a seasoned veteran in the drug world. She knew that a man like Jesus knew how to hide his true objective. His sudden generosity would be very questionable. In a wise person's eyes that knew the tricks and trade of the game.

"You need to be careful with him and everyone in your circle, Fancy. Things can be good now, but when they turn sour, that's when you can't get that taste out of your mouth, because it's gonna be there to stay."

"I'm not you. I can handle this. Can't you just accept that I'm good at what I do and that maybe I'm better than you?" she replied smugly.

Belen sighed heavily. "You just don't understand, little fuckin' girl. This world can get way over your head, and it will eat you alive. And for the record, you could never have done what I did, as good as I did it. I didn't get caught fucking slipping; Alexandro did and took me down with him. Remember that."

Fancy was growing tired of her mother's negative attitude. She uttered with some contempt, "Are you jealous of me? Do you hate what I've accomplished so far?"

"Fancy, jealous? Get it through your thick fuckin' scull that you're no threat. Ever. Not even on a bad day. I'm no fuckin' hater, I love you. I'm your mother. You are my daughter—"

"Then fuckin' act like it and be happy for me, Mother!" Fancy exclaimed. "I can fuckin' do this business!"

She was starting to believe that Belen and Nasir were truly jealous of her. It was becoming a tiresome argument with her mother about her maturity in the game. She frowned heavily, and her last words to her mother before her abrupt departure was, "When I'm done I'm gonna run this city and everything around it. They ain't seen cold until they see and fuck with me."

She made her exit from the prison.

The perks of having money were becoming a supreme goddess in the underworld and being able to afford to do whatever you wanted in life. Having tons of money and wealth made Fancy's access limitless to the finer things in life. She was sitting on a mountain of cash and she wasn't trying to see hard times anymore. Her name was becoming well known in the streets. With Nasir by her side and having her back, and dealing with Jesus, she had killers at her beck and call. Fancy was trafficking drugs from New Jersey to South Carolina under the radar. She had a system set up with moving and tow trucks taking Route 78 to 81, which was through the mountains. The highway had fewer tolls and bridges to cross.

She had been in the game a few months, and so far she hadn't disappointed Jesus or the cartel. But there were a few bumps and bruises to her rise of grace. When someone disrespected her personally or her organization, she sent Nasir and his thugs to handle it. When a crew tried to challenge her in the streets, Nasir came into the picture and handled things his way—violently. When those that received product from her on consignment in or out of state and refused or couldn't pay their debt, she sent Nasir and his goon squad to collect any debt owed to her or send out a strong and nasty statement. Nasir was her sidekick, her lover—also the ferocious pit bull she kept on a leash until it was time to attack. He was her muscle.

Along with Nasir's nasty pedigree came his very violent and deadly goons, Red, Tico, Ozone, and Blowout. Their names were notorious on the streets for spilling blood and breaking limbs.

If there was a problem, Nasir and his thugs handled it. Most times it was really messy.

Fancy sat poolside at her latest Long Island estate. She was getting a pedicure and sipping expensive champagne. At the moment, life was good. She was benefiting from the fruits of her hard labor. Once again she was back to living the life she had grown up with.

She'd already proven that she could stay in her lane and keep up in the race. Since the meeting with Amarillo, she'd moved three hundred thousand kilos in two months, a move that was unprecedented. She definitely had Jesus' attention, and he requested a second meeting with her.

The sun was radiant above, the weather balmy, and the sprawling blue sky was very appealing with it being almost the summer. Clad in a two-piece bikini and stiletto heels, she was the epitome of a diva at her best.

"I like it, Lucy. You are definitely doing your thing with my toes," Fancy said, lifting her toes to get a better look at the pink and white swirled design on her toes. "You got skills, girl."

"Thanks, Fancy," Lucy returned, smiling.

"You are worth every penny."

Fancy admired her pedicure for a moment. The exact details were flawless. She was ready to slide her feet into some open-toed shoes and hit the club tonight. It was always VIP treatment wherever she went.

Fancy reached into her small bag near the chair and handed Lucy, her personal nail tech, a hundred-dollar bill.

"Keep the change," said Fancy.

Lucy was very thankful and happy. She collected her things and made her exit.

Fancy stood up and continued to admire her pedicure. Her body was flawless in the skimpy blue bikini. The pool was blue like the sky and glistening like it had diamonds on the bottom. Her four-bedroom home was a picture of opulence sitting on three acres of land with an in-ground pool nestled in the shaded backyard and offering more than 3,600 square feet of living space along with soaring ceilings, detailed woodwork, and two fireplaces.

Using more brains than brawn, Fancy had studied business, finance, and real estate in her private school. She picked up a few things about business from Alexandro, and mastered the art of setting up shell companies and money laundering to wash and hide the sizable income she suddenly had coming in. Unbeknownst to everyone, including her mother, she teamed up with super lawyer Gary Scheck for other reasons besides her mother's criminal case and appeal, and offered him a healthy business proposition. She felt Nasir wasn't smart enough to understand how that side of the game worked. He was a Brooklyn thug that she loved, but when it came to investing into something financially stable, he was inept.

Fancy surrounded herself with a team of the best financial investors, attorneys, and businessmen in New York. She wasn't a fool like Nasir and other young hustlers who spent their drug money on fancy cars and clothes, heavy jewelry, and bitches. She had a plan for herself. The first thing she did when she started making her millions was put away a nice large nest egg for herself just in case her rainy days did come. As her father had done before her, Fancy had stashed millions of dollars somewhere safe, untouchable until a crisis came.

She enrolled herself into college and created false 1040 tax forms to cover her ass from the IRS. And with the help of Gary, she created a believable income for herself via the shell companies they created and other means. He was very smart when it came to the law and about business. He was the best.

He became her silent partner in a few things. It also helped that Gary Scheck respected her father and was attracted to Fancy. He made sure that Fancy crossed her T's and dotted her I's in every business move she made.

Because she was young, they thought she was naive, but she was far from it. The type of methods Gary used to launder her money were called round-tripping, cash-intensive businesses, and bank capture. It took Fancy a couple weeks to fully understand the process, but she was an A student in her former life and only a fool would invest so much money into something they didn't understand.

Gary Scheck taught her the ropes, and Fancy learned quickly.

Fancy walked away from the pool and headed inside, but before she could make it into her home, Nasir appeared out of nowhere into her yard, startling her.

"Damn-it Nasir, where the fuck did you come from?" she hollered.

"I made it my profession and business to be silent and sneaky," he returned.

"I could have shot you."

Nasir walked toward her and asked, "With what? I always warned you to keep ya pistol close."

He lifted his shirt to show the .9mm tucked in his waistband. Fancy stared at her man and admired his urban attire—dark, long cargo shorts and a white V-neck underneath his spring jacket. He had been working out and looked swelled and fit in many key areas of his body.

Fancy walked up to him, wrapped her arms around her boo, pressed her scantily clad breasts against his chest, and planted the wettest and sweetest kiss against Nasir's lips. They kissed passionately for a moment. Nasir reached around her curvy waist and cupped her juicy ass. The moment was enticing; the feeling for him was tempting.

Fancy stopped the kiss and out of the blue asked him, "Do you feel like taking a road trip?"

"To where?"

"I need you to handle something for me in South Carolina."

"Like what?"

"Something that needs your expertise only. I'm having a problem with a certain muthafucka down there who calls himself Demon."

"Demon?" It was an odd name.

"I know. I have five kilos missing and no reasonable explanation why," Fancy stated. "You are the only one I can trust to make this run and come back with results."

Nasir felt reluctant to make the trip. He had never been to South Carolina. It was a foreign state to him. He wasn't afraid to take the trip; it was too many miles away. He wasn't going alone, though.

"I'll pay you twenty-five thousand for this one, baby. It will be easy money for you."

"When I'm supposed to leave?"

"Tomorrow."

"Thirty thousand."

Fancy chuckled. "Money talks."

"Very clearly," Nasir responded.

"Okay, and I need this done ASAP!"

Nasir didn't care about the money; thirty thousand was peanuts to him. He was making a fortune by partnering with Fancy, being the second in command of her multimillion-dollar criminal empire. But he also liked the thrill of the hunt—the streets were his heart and murder was something he executed very well. It was one thing he controlled, sparing life or meting out death.

And losing five kilos in South Carolina was nothing major to them when they were moving birds by the boatloads and making millions of dollars. But it was the principle of the loss, and Fancy understood if someone got away with it once, then that same person or others wouldn't hesitate to try it again. So she had to make a serious issue of it and make an example out of someone.

And if Fancy had a problem with a man named Demon in South Carolina, then Demon had a serious problem with Nasir in New York.

Nasir gazed at his girl in her sexy bikini and had some impure thoughts. He reached out to kiss his lady again. He desired her greatly. She was such a beautiful woman. He wanted to be inside of her so badly. It had been a minute since they fucked. He sternly gripped Fancy in his arms and tried to undo her bikini top, but she wasn't having it. She pulled away from his hold and replied, "What do you think you're doing?"

"I want you, that's what the fuck I'm doin'," he bluntly replied.

"Now is not the time, Nasir."

"Then when?"

"Nasir, I gave you something to do, and I'm not in the mood."

"I'm supposed to be ya man, not ya fuckin' servant or slave. You need to really remember that, Fancy," he spat.

Fancy frowned, and was about to respond to his boorish remark, but her cell phone rang, taking her attention from Nasir to the caller. It seemed more important than his sexual needs. Fancy dismissed herself from Nasir's stunted rant and walked into her home, leaving Nasir dumbfounded. He frowned, pulled out a cigarette, and made his exit. He didn't like at all how Fancy just treated him, especially when he was killing for her.

CHAPTER 8

Fancy stepped out of the silver Maybach in downtown Manhattan clad in a sexy silver minidress, her open-toed high heels looking amazing. She exuded sexiness and grace, emulating the celebrities that strutted out onto the red carpet of an essential event. She caught fleeting looks and some lingering attention as the suited driver escorted her into the towering steel-and-glass skyscraper standing 60 floors high and stretching into the clouds. The downtown area was bustling with hordes of people up and down the city blocks, and the thick evening traffic made downtown looking like a parking lot with everyone enjoying the lovely spring evening.

Fancy had been summoned to meet with Jesus again, this time in the city—and no Nasir around this time, and no goons. She was excited to meet with the man she knew was her real father. She dressed up lovingly for the meeting and beamed with happiness. Fancy yearned to have a heart-to-heart talk with Jesus. She wanted to get to know him and understand him better. She wanted to become him, and with the success she has been having on the streets, she was well on her way into becoming a significant figure in the crime world.

Fancy followed behind the driver into the elaborate glass and marble lobby. It was like something out of Oz, with the swanky black-and-white marble flooring, colossal ceiling, a spectacular chandelier, and gleaming round pillars that emulated something out of Rome.

She made her way to the elevator and stepped inside alone. The driver of the Maybach didn't proceed. He looked at Fancy and said in his thick, Colombian accent, "You go up alone. I stay here."

Fancy pushed for the top floor. The doors closed and the elevator quickly ascended like a rocket taking off, but it was a smooth ride to the top. She stopped at the top floor and stepped into a world of opulence and grandeur. Fancy walked into a room with floor-to-ceiling windows revealing a 360-degree picturesque view of the city and everything beyond it. The amenities included beautiful parquet flooring, two marble baths, a sauna, and a Sub-Zero refrigerator. Outside, there was a flowing infinite pool that was breathtaking.

Fancy was amazed by it all. She'd had means herself and grew up around many grand things, but living like this was supreme. She was alone in the 2,700-square-foot room and wondered where Jesus was. She walked toward the floor-to-ceiling windows and gazed out at a sprawling metropolis that was about to be lit up with myriad of lights as soon as dusk touched over the city.

"You like the view?" she heard someone say.

Fancy turned to see Jesus entering the room. He was clad in a black, three-piece Armani suit and alligator shoes. He wore a diamond-encrusted Rolex and not another piece of jewelry on his person. He didn't even have his ears pierced. He exemplified power and style. His presence in the room made a hasty difference. His tapered salt-and-pepper cropped hair and thick goatee were well groomed, and his manicured nails were almost better than hers.

"I love it," Fancy replied.

"I do too. It's the reason why I spend so much time in this place. You get to see everything from every direction," Jesus said. "Was the drive from your Long Island residence a comfortable one?"

"It was . . . thanks."

He nodded.

Fancy felt a tinge of nervousness. Being alone in a room with Jesus brought about an uneasy feeling to almost everyone. His eyes could be cold and callous, but his voice was always so calm and trouble-free—but it had a chilling timbre to it also. He stood close to Fancy and stared out the window. His attention was on other towering buildings and the New Jersey skyline. Fancy glanced at him and then looked that way, too.

"I like looking out of windows. I love a beautiful view, especially this kind of view. It brings about such reverence for this city, giving off such a tranquil feeling from far above the ground when down below can be such a rude and noisy place," he stated coolly.

"I know."

Jesus gazed lingered at the sun setting and dusk arriving.

"Do you want a drink?" he asked her.

"Yes . . . please."

Jesus walked over to the bar nestled near the window and poured white wine into two wine glasses. He approached Fancy again and handed her the smooth looking fluid. She downed hers immediately. She wanted more.

"It's Henri Jayer Richebourg Grand Cru, Côte de Nuits, France. Sixteen thousand dollars per bottle," Jesus informed her. "I drink nothing but the best."

"I see."

"You prefer another glass?"

Fancy nodded.

Jesus poured her another glass of wine, and this time she sipped it slowly, savoring the taste, relishing drinking top-notch wine with Jesus. Jesus walked toward the window again and gazed out of it. He took a few sips of wine and without turning to look at Fancy, he said, "You have made some unprecedented moves in the past couple months. I am highly impressed."

"Thank you, Mr. Negro," she returned, remaining calm, but excited about the praise from him on the inside.

"I must admit, I doubted you for a moment, but you prove to me and my men that you were a great choice."

"I was born to do this."

"We are not born to be criminals, but only molded into the people we are because of either survival or our upbringing," Jesus corrected.

It was a shrewd statement from Jesus.

He continued drinking his wine and turned to look at Fancy. Fancy wanted to ask him so many questions, but she was in no position to do so. It made her curious as to why he had called for her.

"Tell me about yourself, Rojo," said Jesus.

"What do you want to know?"

"Entertain me for the moment."

Fancy thought for a moment. What could she tell this man that he probably didn't already know about her? Should she be up front about everything, including her knowing that she was his daughter? Should she lie? He had eyes and ears everywhere. Maybe it was a trick for her to confess, or maybe it wasn't.

Fancy sighed and said to him, "I grew up privileged, Mr. Negro, and of course, you already know who my parents were . . . especially my mother. But the life I lived with my parents was a lie. I thought they were legit and honest parents operating a multimillion-dollar business. So imagine my surprise when the FBI came raiding our home and arresting my mother and father. I was so adamant that it had to be a mistake—my parents weren't criminals—but when the truth gradually started to reveal itself, I was so lost. And we lost everything, Mr. Negro. I had to learn quick and fast, and overnight I became an outcast to friends and family.

"I went to live with my aunt in Brooklyn who hated me, and the man, my lover who I thought was my cousin, turned out not to be. But I became a killer because of him. And I also felt betrayed because of him. I felt betrayed by so many people that I trusted."

Jesus listened quietly.

Fancy talked, and the more she revealed to Jesus about things that happened to her since the FBI raid, the more watery her eyes became. It felt like she was talking to a therapist and finally spilling out all of her pain and suffering. Jesus wanted to know more about her; well she was giving it to him in the particulars. Fancy didn't know why or where it came from—maybe the fact that this was her real biological father made her feel comfortable talking to him. She wanted to cry on his shoulder and be hugged by him. But Jesus remained distant and unreadable.

"But I'm proving to everyone that I'm not weak and naive, and now, look what I've built and accomplished," she said gruffly.

"You have come a long way," replied Jesus.

Jesus eyed her for a long moment. She was a beautiful young woman— any man's fantasy. He truly admired her perseverance and structure. She was very intelligent and ambitious.

"I see you have invested your money into a few companies and aligned yourself with Gary Scheck," he said, while making his way back to the bar for another drink.

Fancy was surprised that he knew about her attorney's name and more importantly, about her investments.

Jesus noticed the staggered look on Fancy's face when he mentioned Gary Scheck.

"Yes, I'm a very familiar with your attorney. He's astute and very adept when it comes to business and criminal cases. It's a wonder he hadn't represented your parents' case."

"Shit went to hell very fast, and money became sparse," she replied.

"But now he plays for your team."

"Yes, he does."

Jesus smiled. It was the only smile from him for the night. Fancy was playing chess and she was about to scream out checkmate against her mother and so many others that doubted and defied her.

"I admire your bravado, and your honesty. But you still have a lot to learn about this life," he said.

Fancy wanted to scream out, Then teach me! But she didn't, remaining composed and nodding.

Jesus had not summoned Fancy just to converse about her past life. He also wanted a personal update from her about what was going on with his product. It was something he rarely did, but Fancy was an exception. She explained to him where everything was being shipped to, and the minor problems she'd run into, but were quickly taken care of.

"I handle things quickly, Mr. Negro. No matter how big or small it is, I give it my full attention before it becomes a greater threat to me," she stated. "I've learned that prevention is always better than the cure."

Jesus liked what he heard. He nodded. "So right, Rojo."

He walked over to a small late Georgian mahogany serving table with a lovely old wax finish and opened the bottom drawer, pulling out a box of Cuban cigars. Jesus inspected and sniffed the cigar, cut the tip off, and lit it with technique. He took a few strong pulls from it and exhaled the smoke into the air. It was the thing he loved, cigars.

He talked to Fancy for a short moment, enjoying the flavorsome cigar and then approached her with his eyes glazed with some admiration for the young, angelic-looking beauty that had a heart like ice, but intelligence like some Wall Street tycoon.

Jesus reached out and gently touched her hair, admiring the smooth texture of it. His touch was almost inappropriate and creepy with him being her father, which Fancy found uncomfortable to deal with. But

Jesus made no advances toward her. His lingering stare did cause her to become uneasy. But he took a few steps back from her and said, "You are something else, Rojo . . . a diamond in a rough. Your foes underestimate you, and that is always a grave mistake."

She didn't respond to him. Jesus was a very intriguing individual filled with riddles and mysteries. The two talked for a moment until Jesus told her their meeting was done.

"I'm a very busy man, Rojo, and unfortunately, my time is valuable. I enjoyed our talk, but my servant will escort you out, and my driver will take you back to your location," he said in a courteous tone.

Fancy understood. The small amount of time she got to spend with him was pleasurable and useful. He had other important business to take care of. He had gotten his update and was satisfied with the report.

A tall man dressed in a black suit all of a sudden appeared out of nowhere like a phantom and gazed at Fancy with his straight face. She made her way toward the exit while Jesus went into the neighboring room. When she got back on the elevator, her heart dropped like the elevator descending. She missed having a father in her life, someone to protect her and always be there for her. She was looking for that from Jesus for some strange reason, but he seemed detached and reserved. He talked to her, but it was far from how Alexandro used to converse with her.

Fancy stepped off the elevator and into the street. The back door of the silver Maybach was already opened for her to climb inside. The driver was standing there, ready to usher her inside and drive her wherever she needed to go. Everything seemed so prearranged for her.

As the Maybach headed north on the FDR Drive, Fancy started to smoke a cigarette and gaze out the window, seeing the city going by. The only thing she could think about was Jesus. She wanted to feel that fatherly love again.

CHAPTER 9

Nasir opened his eyes and saw the sign that said WELCOME TO SOUTH CAROLINA. It was a twelve-hour drive from New York, and he had slept for four hours straight. They were roughly forty-five miles from Greenville, South Carolina, their intended destination. The sun was fresh in the sky, and the warm weather was welcoming to the two men in the rented Dodge Charger with New Jersey plates riding south on I-85.

Nasir yawned and gazed at the thick line of trees to his right and the highway sparse with cars in the early morning hour. They both were foreign to the southern, Republican, redneck state and were armed with a few automatic pistols. They came for business and didn't care for the sightseeing. They wanted to be back in New York as soon as possible. The country was a different playing field from the world they came from.

"How far are we from Greenville?" Nasir asked.

"Sign said about forty miles," Red replied.

"Damn, that long huh? Shit, nigga, stop and get us sumthin' to eat then, cuz I'm fuckin' hungry," Nasir said.

"I saw a sign that said there was a Waffle House comin' up," said Red.

"Nigga, what the fuck is a Waffle House?"

"A place that sells waffles, I guess," Red replied, being dumbfounded by it. "I mean, it's breakfast shit, right?"

"Fuck it, stop there then and we get sumthin' to eat. My stomach is growling like a muthafucka."

"A'ight."

Nasir removed his pack of Newports and lit a cigarette. He needed his early morning nicotine. He exhaled the smoke, took a few more pulls, and shared the cigarette with Red. Nasir couldn't believe Fancy was sending him way down to the South to kill some country, slow bumpkin for five ki's. Yeah, they had to set a violent example, but his time could have been used for other important matters.

The Charger drove down the highway doing 80 mph, the stereo bumping Wu-Tang, and the cigarette smoke filling up the ride.

"We don't even have a picture of this nigga," Nasir complained. "These southern niggas may all look alike to me. And for all we know this nigga Fulton we 'posed to meet that's expected to point out Demon could point out the wrong muthafucka!"

"We gonna find him, Nasir. Small town, small thinkin' muthafuckas. How hard can it be? We connected to the cartel right? So niggas already gonna fear us. We say who we are, let these bitches know what we about early, spread out some cash, and the nigga gonna get got. And then we back in New York fuckin' bitches," Red proclaimed.

Yeah, it sounded like an easy plan, but Nasir had a feeling that it wasn't going to be that simple. But he was ready to roll with it. They had nothing else to run with.

Red exited at the next exit that advertised the Waffle House, and a few other restaurants, along with some gas stations. The road winded into a small town that seemed tranquil and easygoing. There wasn't any bustling traffic, hordes of pedestrians moving about, or any long streets lined with shops and businesses. Everything seemed so spread out and distanced from each other.

Nasir looked around and couldn't believe how quiet things were around him. He was reclined in the passenger seat and somewhat in awe that he was in the South. He was a city boy, and the country was no place for him.

"There it go right there." Red pointed out.

The quaint eatery looking structure nestled off the main road was ahead of them. They gazed up at the towering sign that read in bright bold, yellow letters, WAFFLE HOUSE.

"So this is a Waffle House," said Nasir.

"You think they food is any good?" asked Red.

"Fuck it, let's find out."

They parked and stepped out of the Charger and walked toward the place. They both were ready to feast on some southern cooked meal. Beside their Charger, there was an old, dusty, beat-up pickup truck in the parking lot.

The two New Yorkers stepped into the quaint diner and the employees and sole customer inside already determined that they were out-of-towners from their urban attire, New York ball caps, and their northern accents.

"Good mornin' 'n' welcome to the Waffle House, fellows," the slim, uniformed waitress greeted jovially.

The men were unsmiling; they greeted the employees with a head nod and took a seat at the booth near the window. Nasir looked around. A waitress came over to service them. She greeted them with a warm smile and a gentle hello.

"Can I get y'all fellows somethin' to drink . . . coffee, tea?" she asked in her southern accent.

Nasir sized her up quickly. Young, poor, white woman, slim, long brown hair pulled back into a ponytail, raggedy nails, chipped polish. And her affable persona seemingly genuine. She had the pen and pad in her hand and was ready to take their orders.

Red was the first to order. "Yeah, let me get a cup of coffee."

"And you, sir?"

"I'll have the same."

She jotted down their order.

"So, where y'all from?" she asked kindly.

Nasir and Red chuckled lightly. The look in her young eyes showed that she was highly intrigued by the two men's thuggish demeanor. But the two weren't too keen on entertaining her or telling their business to strangers.

"Up north," Nasir replied dryly.

"Up north, like New York up north?"

"What are you, a cop?" Nasir replied coolly.

She laughed and innocently uttered, "Oh, heck no. I just ain't never been out of South Carolina that's all, and only being friendly. And we don't get too many people from out of town in here."

"Some words of advice, love. Sometimes it's good to let strangers be strangers, and just do ya job," Nasir said bluntly.

She looked stunned by his comment, replied with an apology for her intrusiveness, and walked away to fulfill their orders. They stared at the menus and saw a decent selection to order from.

"Fuckin' Mayberry out this place," Nasir said. "I keep waiting for Andy Griffith to walk in this bitch."

Red laughed.

They were armed with their pistols tucked snugly in their waistbands, not knowing what to expect. The staff was lightweight: one male cook and two waitresses. And the customer seated on the other side was a dusty looking old man in a dingy blue hat, cowboy boots, and worn jeans. It was obvious that the dusty pickup truck parked outside belonged to him. Anyone else didn't seem to be a threat, so the men relaxed a little.

The waitress came back with their coffees and to take their food orders. Both men ordered the All-Star breakfast. For the duration of their meal, they talked about business up north, being in the South, and Fancy.

"Shit is goin' to her fuckin' head, Red. I swear the other fuckin' day at our crib she treated me like I was her manservant or fuckin' sumthin. I ain't her personal bitch," Nasir let his feelings be known. "I lay down niggas for her and she gonna talk to me some kinda way."

"She's the boss now, Nasir. She got the cartel backing her and us. We making a shit load of money. What can we do?" Red said. "And besides, ain't that ya girl?"

Nasir sighed and thought about it. Fancy was his woman, but lately he hadn't been feeling like it was a relationship between them—it was like a dictatorship. They were supposedly coming up together, building an empire, but he had more blood on his hands than a militant soldier in Sierra Leone while she was enjoying the good life.

"Things need to change, Red."

"How?"

"I don't know yet, but I'm tired of Fancy thinkin' she a god in these streets after only a few months. It's because of me she got this far."

Red took a bite out of the large waffle in front of him and somewhat agreed to what Nasir was saying to him.

"Yo, these waffles good as fuck," said Red, while chewing with his mouth open.

He was only a thug following orders. He killed for a profit, and he was satisfied with his position. But Nasir wanted so much more. After a few bites from his meal, he suddenly lost his appetite. He thought about his future, and it didn't seem as bright as he wanted it to be.

They finished their meal, paid the bill, and left the white, affable waitress a twenty-dollar tip. She was shocked by it. Before his exit, Nasir turned and winked at the girl, and walked out. She smiled.

The two men climbed into the car and drove the forty miles into Greenville.

Greenville was a southern, small, but uplifting city nestled in upstate South Carolina that was becoming a growing city with jobs, businesses and an increasing economy after the recession, but it also was having its fair share of drugs and crime.

After checking into a cheap Motel 6, showering, getting some much-needed rest, and changing clothes, Nasir and Red walked into a darkened bar called Swagg off I-85. The two immediately stood out in the place like a Muslim at a KKK rally. They couldn't hide that they were from out of town, New York exactly, and they looked like trouble.

A few of the ladies took an interest in Nasir and Red, and the local thugs gave them some side stares and a few hard looks as they went to the bar to order their drinks. Nasir felt the tension, but he wasn't worried about it. It appeared that locals didn't take too kindly to hard-looking strangers suddenly appearing in their bar.

Nasir took a swig from his beer and started to smoke a cigarette. He eyed every face in the bar and sized up everyone. The pistol was concealed on him, the safety already off. The hunt had already begun. Demon, who the fuck was Demon and why didn't they have a face for him? he thought. They were supplying this small town with several kilos a week. They had a man in the city named Fulton. He was their guy in the South.

Fulton was supposed to meet the men at Swagg and point out Demon to them. Supposedly he was this badass gun slinger; a killer and a drug dealer with a fierce reputation in the city, and he was putting a serious dent in the drug traffic there.

Trinidad James blared throughout the place. The dance floor was swelling with a crowd performing the latest dance moves. The ladies were thick, country and looking luscious in their tight jeans and short skirts. Red was ready to snatch one up and take her back to his room and fuck her brains out. But business came first. He downed his beer and was ready to get into some action.

"Where is this clown?" Red asked.

Nasir looked at the time. It was 11 pm. Fulton was a half-hour late, and the bar Swagg seemed to be the kind of place they didn't want to hang around for too long. Nasir made conversation with the female bartender who seemed to have an interest in him. He entertained her with small talk while keeping vigilant of his unfamiliar surroundings.

While Red went off to use the bathroom, Nasir smoked a Newport and drank his beer. From his peripheral vision he noticed Fulton walking into the bar, flanked by two country-looking goons. Fulton only stood five-seven and was decorated with heavy jewelry and a throwback Cowboys jersey. He locked eyes with Nasir, recognizing him right away, and walked over.

The first thing out of Fulton's mouth was an apology. "Nasir, tell Fancy I'm sorry for the fuckup, and I'm tryin' to make it right wit' her. It ain't my fault 'bout da five birds missing. But this dude Demon, he's a muthafuckin' problem down here."

Fulton's accent was heavy. He had a chubby face and a bald head. He seemed nervous. Nasir immediately sized him up and didn't respond to the apology. He took another drink from his beer and finally responded calmly with, "Let's have this talk outside . . . less people around to listen."

When Nasir stepped away from the bar, Red was returning from the bathroom. He saw Fulton and his goons and didn't trust anyone in the South. He followed behind Nasir outside with his hand close to his pistol. One wrong move and he was going to start blazing. But unbeknownst to everyone, another set of eyes in the spot were watching Nasir and Red leave out of the darkened bar with Fulton and his men. The harrowing figure downed his drink and went through a different exit.

Outside, Nasir and Red had a talk with Fulton next to his bright red Jaguar sitting on chromed rims. His young goons stood off in the distance minding their business. Fulton was the main dude in Greenville with a violent history, but he truly humbled himself in front of Nasir, understanding his clout with the Colombian cartel.

"Who the fuck is this Demon and where can we find him?" Nasir asked.

"He kinda hard to find," Fulton replied.

"What you mean hard to find? From what I see, Greenville ain't that big of a city for someone to hide in," Nasir barked.

"He like Omar from *The Wire*, just be poppin' up outta nowhere and takin' niggas' shit—making his money from other niggas' product. And he got a gang of goons that are wild 'n' shit," Fulton proclaimed.

"And what you think we are down here, the fuckin' Mickey Mouse Club?" Nasir barked. "First, who do you know that's connected to this muthafucka, and where do you think we can find him?"

"He usually frequents this spot called the Dugout."

"And where's this spot at?"

"I'll take you there."

It was all Nasir needed to hear. Everyone jumped into their cars and headed toward the Dugout, a hood sports bar nestled in the backwoods of Greenville. It was a five-minute ride on the other side of the highway.

"You think they tryin' to play us?" Red asked.

"They better not be," Nasir replied.

They parked on a side dirt road next to a dozen other cars. When the men got out, Fulton and his men were already waiting for them in the parking lot.

Fulton walked up to Nasir and said, "I'ma let y'all know right now that they search for weapons before you step inside."

It was a problem for Nasir and Red. They weren't about to give up their weapons and become vulnerable in the country. He frowned. They were too far from home and with it being just the two of them, they had to watch each other backs.

"Red, you stay out here, Fulton and I will go inside and look around for this fool," he said.

Red nodded.

He gave his pistol for Red to hold. And then he walked into the Dugout behind Fulton. The blaring music and large crowd wasn't anything new to Nasir. An NBA game was playing on several mounted flat screens positioned around the bar. The bar was crowded with customers and the three females bartenders were very busy taking drink orders.

Nasir moved through the place like he owned it. He had attention on him like he was a celebrity. Fulton greeted a few people he knew, but he didn't have time to socialize. They walked toward the back where a few men were playing pool. Fulton looked around, but there wasn't any sign of Demon or his minions.

"He ain't here," Fulton said.

Nasir frowned heavily. He didn't have time to go wandering around the city looking for one problem.

"Where else you think he might be?" he asked.

"Like I said before, this nigga be ghost like that."

Fulton wasn't much help. Nasir started to doubt him greatly— maybe he was part of the setup, the reason why five ki's were taken from the organization. If so, he was already a dead man. The men exited the Dugout and met up with their triggermen outside. Nasir looked at Red and he couldn't hide the frustration on his face. The longer they spent in Greenville, South Carolina, the more agitated they became. They hoped to be on the highway back to New York tomorrow sometime.

"It's still early; we got other places to look around," said Fulton.

It felt like they were going on a wild goose chase. Nasir lit a cigarette and puffed out the smoke. He retrieved his gun back from Red and walked toward the car. Fulton suggested they attend a place called Pot Belly's on

Augusta Road. It was where a lot of hustlers went to unwind and meet some fine women.

"We go here, and he ain't there, then we tax this loss on you, Fulton. And it ain't gonna be fuckin' pretty. We don't have all night chasing for a fuckin' Demon . . . we ain't priests," Nasir said pointedly.

Fulton didn't like what was just said. He kept his composure and assured them they were going to find the problem. Nasir decided to drive. Their Charger was parked directly next to Fulton's bright red Jaguar. Nasir was about to climb into the Charger but something immediately caught his attention. He noticed an Impala with an elaborate candy paint job, tinted windows, and 22-inch chromed rims approaching slowly. He eyed the car, but before he could come to his street senses, windows came rolling down and the barrel of an Uzi machine gun and a .9mm came thrusting out and loud gunfire erupted.

Tat! Tat! Tat! Tat! Tat! Tat! Tat! Tat!
Bak! Bak! Bak! Bak! Bak!

Everyone quickly took cover from the gunfire. Nasir hit the ground and caught a few scrapes and bruises as he pulled out his .9mm. He crouched near the back of his car and was ready to return fire. He could hear the bullets ripping through the metal and glass shattering. He could hear people screaming.

The Impala took off, tires screeching, making a sharp turn and disappeared hastily into the dark. Nasir quickly got up and rushed out into the street. He wanted to see which way the car went, but it was too late.

"That was him . . . that was Demon," Fulton exclaimed.

Nasir scowled. He hated that he missed his shot. He hated that someone had gotten the better of him and almost took his life. These country bumpkins weren't that slow after all. He had been caught slipping—someone had been watching them since they arrived, or telling on them.

"Oh shit!" someone shouted.

Nasir turned and saw the shock. Red had been shot in the neck. He was sprawled out on his back and bleeding profoundly. He squirmed around in the dirt, moaning and holding his bloody wound to try and stop some of the bleeding. He was still alive and breathing, but barely. Nasir rushed over to him and tried to aid him.

"Just remain calm, Red . . . stay calm," Nasir cried out. His hands became covered with Red's blood.

Red gazed up at Nasir with pleading eyes. He couldn't speak, but his petrified look expressed that he didn't want to die. His gaze toward Nasir was gradually fading. A small crowd gathered around the incident. This infuriated Nasir. He screamed, "Y'all back the fuck up! Back the fuck up!"

His voice roared out, but they barely moved. Nasir was just a man—a face in Greenville.

"Nas, police 'bout to be on they way, man. We need to go," Fulton exclaimed with his heavy accent.

Nasir didn't want to leave Red. He was dying. Red was the only man he trusted in the South. Nasir's face was covered with rage and anguish. They had been in South Carolina less than twenty-four hours and already shit done went bad. Nasir stood up. Red's eyes were closed. He was gone. Nasir was alone. He turned and glared at Fulton. This had to be a setup. He lifted his gun toward Fulton's direction and was tempted to fire. The crowd around gasped, but still refused to move.

"It wasn't me, Nasir! I promise you that! It was Demon! And believe me we all are sick of this muthafucka!" Fulton shouted heatedly.

Nasir continued to glare at Fulton.

"You better pray we find this muthafucka, Fulton, because one phone call back to New York and this entire city will feel a biblical wrath come down on it in a fuckin' heartbeat," Nasir growled through his clenched teeth with his nostrils flaring.

"I won't rest until he's dead," Fulton replied.

Nasir jumped into the Charger, leaving Red dead on the ground, and they fled the crime scene minutes before Greenville police arrived.

CHAPTER 10

Fancy looked at her new shoes in awe. Like most women she had a shoe fetish and her new stilettos were eye candy. The Christian Louboutin heels she had on cost $5,000, and the bling she wore was blinding. Fancy took comfort in partying in the lavish VIP area of club Oasis in midtown Manhattan. Despite the tight security detail around her, she was alone in the spacious VIP area with a bottle of chilled Moët to drink. She limberly moved to the sound of John Hart's "Who Booty" blaring throughout the large and vibrant club packed with hundreds of patrons.

Briefly she thought about Nasir. Sending him to South Carolina was her smartest move. She wanted a break from him and decided to test how well he could handle himself in the South. It was where a majority of their kilos were being shipped—North Carolina, South Carolina and Georgia were her best states. Business was so good in the South that she was thinking about having Nasir set up shop and create a central hub there.

With Nasir in South Carolina, she needed to occupy her time. Clubbing used to be a big thing she loved to do before her world fell apart with the FBI raid at her home. She and her ex-best friend, Rosario, used to sneak off to the clubs when they were young—lying to their parents about spending the night at each other's houses and then dressing up in their sexiest attire, pulling out their fake I.D.'s, and partying in some of the city's elite nightclubs.

Rosario was now a memory, and Fancy was a boss bitch. She took a sip of Moët straight from the bottle. She didn't care for a glass. It was her world, her rules, and she lived life her way. She could buy the club if she wanted; she was that paid. She stood up and moved to the DJ's banging mixes and walked toward the railing that overlooked the crowd below. Isolated and perched above, she appeared to be a goddess to everyone below with her raven-black hair flowing and impeccable beauty.

Fancy stared at a few faces mixed in the crowd, but one particular person caught her direct attention and she didn't know why. The exotic-looking woman moved on the dance floor seductively and with elegance. She had rhythm and such a magnetic sex appeal that even women gawked at her, too. It seemed a crowd was flocking around her. But what caught Fancy's attention was that she was wearing the same Anthony Vaccarello black and gold dress that Gisele Bündchen wore to the Met gala a few months back. She had a body to fit the dress perfectly with her protruding ass and big tits. Her hair was just as long as Fancy's, and her attitude seemed fierce. Fancy wasn't a lesbian, but she found this particular female to be very attractive.

With her eyes fixed on the intriguing woman, Fancy downed the Moët bottle and leaned over the railing. The two ladies locked eyes, and Fancy made it clearly known that she had her attention. The mystery woman smiled, remained nonchalant, and partied like a rock star on the dance floor—and she seemed to have as much swag as Fancy did.

"Who is this bitch?" Fancy asked herself.

The sexy mystery woman continued to entertain herself and others on the floor. She danced, creating some kind of spark inside the club, and then afterwards, she moved through the crowd like she was a boss bitch and went to the bar. Fancy was to some extent hypnotized by the domineering persona in the club. She went over to one of her goons and whispered something in his ear. He nodded and left the VIP area.

Ten minutes later, her towering goon came walking back into the area with the mystery woman following behind him. Fancy stood up and walked over to her. They stared at each other. The woman was even sexier up close. She seemed to be of Hispanic descent, possibly Mexican.

Fancy bluntly asked, "First off, to let you know, I'm not a fuckin' lesbian. I just admire your style down there and decided to invite you into the VIP with me."

"No offense taken. I'm glad you noticed me," she replied. "What's your name?"

"Fancy."

"Nice to meet you. I'm Pippa."

"Unusual name."

"I'm an unusual person," Pippa said with a smile.

"I can see that."

The two walked over to the red velvet seats and sat down. Fancy offered Pippa some Moët, and she accepted gracefully. The bubbly was poured into a short-stemmed glass, and Pippa downed it like it was water. Fancy poured her another glass.

"Where you from, Pippa?" Fancy asked.

"Miami," she answered.

"I love Miami. I've been there a handful of times. South Beach is paradise to me," Fancy said.

"It's a beautiful city. It's paradise to me, too. I love everything about it, from the beaches to the boutique shops," said Pippa.

"I feel you. I know you're familiar with Chanel in Bel Harbour."

"You haven't lived in Miami until you shopped in that store," Pippa replied.

Fancy agreed.

The two women went on to talk about other stores in Miami like the Versace store, Gucci, Tom Ford, and a few other high-end places that only the affluent frequented. Fancy deduced Pippa had wealth of her own. The bling she wore, the clutch purse, and the outfit few could afford. They had so much in common—clothes, shoes, cars, men, and their looks. Fancy had been surrounded by men for months, and for once, it felt good to find a female she could relate to—someone to talk to who was on her level. It was becoming lonely at the top. Pippa didn't seem like a hater, but Fancy also wasn't a fool, and she didn't put too much trust into strangers. She was trying to read Pippa. So far, she seemed cool.

Besides Rosario, whom Fancy felt betrayed by, she hadn't had a girlfriend in years.

"So what brings you to New York?" Fancy asked.

"Business and pleasure. First it's business with him, and then I give him the pleasure," Pippa joked.

Fancy laughed.

"Are you an escort?" Fancy inquired.

Pippa chuckled. "Nah, not my cup of tea, sweetheart."

"Then what do you do? If you don't mind me asking," Fancy said.

"Look at you, just met me and you all in the Kool-Aid," said Pippa.

Fancy chuckled.

"Excuse me; it's just a habit of mine. One can't be too careful who she associates herself with," said Fancy.

"I understand. I'm the same way. And if you don't mind me asking, what do you do? What line of business are you in?"

"I asked first."

"Yes, you did," Pippa replied with a smile.

She took a sip of Moet and gazed at Fancy. She could tell Fancy was a hardball person—a gangstress—the head bitch in charge. The goons surrounding her were evidence of her power.

"Well, to be honest, I'm a boss bitch in Miami. I move those birds, lots of them, and I have a shit load of clientele."

Fancy nodded. She was taken aback that a stranger would be so forthcoming. The question was, is this bitch a cop? Fancy gazed at Pippa heavily and took a sip of Moet.

Pippa read the look and said, "I'm no cop, if that's what you're thinking."

"I never said you were."

"As long as we have that understanding," Pippa protested.

"Who are you here with?"

"I came alone."

"Lookin' like that?" Fancy looked at her jewels and knew that the Brooklyn stick-up kids were thirsty for the next Jux. And if she wasn't careful, she'd be their next victim.

"I have protection." Pippa said firmly.

Fancy nodded.

"Now that I showed you mine, won't you show me yours?"

Fancy remained silent.

"Come on. What's the big secret?"

"It's no secret. I do marketing and publicity for celebrity clients."

"Bullshit," Pippa challenged. "That's fuckin' bullshit."

"What? It's true."

Pippa shook her head and smirked.

Fancy's ego was bursting at the seams wanting to brag and spill the beans, but the cautious side of her was telling her it could be a grave error. She leaned back into the cushioned velvet chair, crossed her legs into a different position, and wrapped her arms around the back of the cushioned seat. She poised herself into a cozy position and stared at this woman who called herself Pippa. She wondered if it was smart to reveal her business to a complete stranger. There weren't any red flags, but sometimes you ran into great liars—hence her parents. And if there was one thing Alexandro drilled into her head, it was that foes could come in many faces—even one as stunningly beautiful as Pippa's.

"I'm a heavy distributor for the cartel," Fancy said straightforwardly, her ego winning.

"Impressive."

"And if you do what you say you do, then maybe we can talk business," said Fancy.

"Oh, I'm definitely the woman I proclaimed to be. My background is nothing to sneeze at, and I have clout with many powerful people. And I'm looking for a new connect. We can definitely talk."

"We might, and we will. But enough about business. You're in New York and we are some fine-ass bitches who are about their paper, so what you say? You ready to cut loose and turn this bitch out?"

"Girl, you ain't saying anything but a word," Pippa replied excitedly.

She stood up, and so did Fancy. Jay-Z blared through the club and the two divas danced like they were good friends. They partied in the club and drank Moët like it was water.

But as the night progressed, Fancy wanted to know more about her newfound friend, and find out why was she so easy to befriend in the first place. She planned on vetting her and placing her peoples on the job right away.

After 3 am, the ladies left club Oasis together after a fantastic night of partying. They continued conversing and exchanged numbers. Fancy was flanked by three of her bodyguards. Pippa strutted through to her car like a bad-ass bitch in heels. The two eye-candies were magnets for attention, but they seemed unfazed by anyone or anything.

Pippa walked toward a gleaming, parked Mercedes Benz CLS63. It was an impressive car. She hit the alarm to her car and gave Fancy a hug goodbye.

"We'll talk, Fancy. I have your number and you have mine," she said. Fancy only nodded.

Pippa climbed into her car and started the ignition. Fancy watched her drive away and took down her license plate number. The first thing tomorrow, she was going to investigate Pippa and see if she was really the woman she proclaimed to be.

Fancy turned to one of her goons and said to him, "If this bitch ain't legit like she says she is, lullaby her ass."

The man nodded. He would be proud to execute the order.

Pippa knew how to deceive someone easily. It was her world. She knew the tricks and trade of infiltrating someone's trust and organization. She knew plenty of computer hackers who forged passports, out-of-state driver's licenses, birth and even death certificates, and many other fraudulent rackets. She had made a career out of being everyone except for herself. Fancy was smart, but she wasn't that smart. She was still a little girl in Pippa's eyes, playing in a grown-up world that would easily chew her up and spit her out. It wasn't going to take long for her to extract revenge.

She expected Fancy to take down her license plate and scrutinize her. Unbeknownst to Fancy, Pippa had been watching her for several weeks now, studying and learning everything about her. She knew her movements and tried to be aware of everything about her, from her social life to her business life.

One flaw Pippa saw about Fancy was that she seemed lonely. Even with Nasir around, Fancy still seemed aloof—secluded from so many things. So Pippa decided the perfect way to infiltrate was to simply befriend Fancy—catch her attention and pretend to have the same attitude and likes as her. And then talk business, because everyone always wanted to make money. The unknown was that Fancy would befriend her first.

Pippa traveled back to her hotel room in downtown, Manhattan. She got on her cell phone and called her friend. The phone rang several times before a woman's voice picked up.

"Hello?"

"Yeah, it's me. I'm inside, the bitch took to me easily," Pippa said.

"Nice . . . She took the bait, huh?"

"Yes she did. But the thing is, she came at me, not the other way around."

"Cuz you a bad bitch, Esmeralda."

"I am, but she's going to see how bad of a bitch I am once I'm through with her and her father. And then I'm gonna make her scream for mercy."

CHAPTER 11

It was Nasir's fourth day in Greenville, South Carolina, and he was beyond tired of hunting for Demon. Demon seemed to be a ghost—no one knew anything. They were either protecting him or truly feared him.

Nasir spread some cash for information on his foe and looked around from county to county—Anderson, Mauldin, Woodruff, and even as far north as Spartanburg for Demon, but to no avail. But Nasir wasn't leaving until the man was dead. He refused to be outsmarted by a country nigga. His ego and pride were on the line, and he wanted revenge for Red. Now things were personal.

He would call New York to check on Fancy and give her an update, but lately she'd been too busy to talk to him. Their conversations were sparse and sometimes curtailed. He didn't even get to tell Fancy about Red's death. He felt that something was going on, and once he was back in New York, he would get to the bottom of it.

The frustration was growing profoundly inside of him, and to temporarily take his mind off the problem, he indulged himself in some female company at his motel room. Sprawled out on his back, butt naked, with beads of sweat forming on his smooth black skin, Nasir moaned as the pair of glossy, luscious lips wrapped around his thick cock and slid down to the base of his dick effortlessly. She glided them up and back down again. Softly, gently, she licked him. She was giving indescribable pleasure with her mouth.

"Suck that dick," Nasir uttered.

He closed his eyes and shut out the outside world for a moment. He gripped her thick light brown hair, cradled the back of her head, and pushed her face farther into his lap. The redbone cutie with the mountain ass and petite tits enveloped all of him with her mouth. She licked every inch of his hard cock as his breathing got louder and louder. Lights danced around in Nasir's head as her slim fingers folded around his fleshy, thick meat with her sweet lips sucking on the tip of his dick as she jerked and sucked him off simultaneously.

"Damn, you got a big dick," she praised in her thick, country accent.

Since coming to the South, it was the one pleasurable moment Nasir had to himself. He had to get Red out of his head and try to forget about the shooting. He had to find some release, and he was about to in the slut he'd picked up from the club a few short hours ago. She was willing to participate in anything Nasir had planned.

She groaned and moaned on the dick she sucked. Nasir gyrated his hips and was ready to explode inside her mouth. She tortured him with her tongue coiled around his dick and her saliva saturating every inch of him. It was bliss. He shut his eyes tightly and concentrated on busting a nut. The feel of her wet, warm mouth and the softness of her lips sliding against him sensually made his eyelids flicker.

Nasir was ready to come, but his ringing and vibrating cell phone on the nightstand prevented him from releasing. He didn't want to answer it, but he figured it could be an important call.

He pulled his dick from the redbone's mouth and pushed her away, reaching over for his cell phone and checking the caller I.D. It was Fulton. Nasir answered right away.

"What?" he uttered.

"We found him, Nasir," Fulton said.

Nasir perked up from the bed and sat upright. It was news that Nasir was waiting to hear. "Where is he?"

"One of my peoples spotted him in Spartanburg. He's lying low at some bitch's crib. I heard he's heavily armed, too . . . knows we been lookin' for him."

"I'm on my way now," Nasir said.

He hung up. His interests were now elsewhere. He reached for his clothing, completely forgetting about the naked redbone in his motel room. He picked up the .9mm Beretta on the table and checked the ammunition. It was fully loaded.

"You not gonna finish ya business wit' me?" she asked. "We were just startin' to have some fun."

Nasir snatched her clothing and purse from off the floor and brusquely tossed it at her.

She didn't seem too pleased by Nasir's handling of her things, but seeing the gun in his hand and the sudden change in his demeanor made her rethink cursing him out.

Nasir dressed hurriedly, stuffed the pistol into his jeans, and grabbed the girl by her arm, because she was taking too long to get dressed. He pushed her toward the door halfway decent.

"Damn nigga, you ain't gotta be so fuckin' rough after I do you a fuckin' favor and just finished suckin' ya dick. I ain't even fuckin' done dressing yet," she spat.

"Yeah, you are! Now shut the fuck up and just leave!" he cursed.

He pushed her out the door and exited the motel room too. Nasir pivoted toward his car and climbed inside, leaving the girl fuming. He climbed into his burgundy Cadillac rental and started it up. Soon, he was on the I-85 highway on his way to Spartanburg. He was itching for revenge and to make an example out of Demon. Four days in South

Carolina was too long for him, and he was ready to go back to New York ASAP after this hit.

Fulton was sitting on the hood of his Jaguar in the Bi-Lo parking lot talking to one of his boys while waiting for Nasir to show up. Forty minutes had gone by since he called him. He smoked a cigarette and wanted to get everything over with.

Fulton saw the Cadillac turning into the parking lot. He took one last pull from the cigarette and flicked it away.

"Let's get this shit over with," he said to his boy.

He removed himself from the hood of his car, standing upright, and kept his eye on the car. It came to a stop and Nasir got out. He approached Fulton and sternly asked, "Where is this nigga?"

"Not too far from hurr. He held up in some trailer park wit' some bitch and his peoples."

It was all Nasir needed to hear.

"Show me the way," he said.

Fulton gazed at Nasir with awe. "You not gonna make a phone call, get some of ya peoples down hurr to handle this?"

"Don't need to," Nasir growled.

"What are you, the Terminator?"

"Just show me the fuckin' way, Fulton."

Fulton tried not to show his fear, but it was manifested through his speech and body language. It was suicide to go against Demon with only three men in a trailer park that they knew nothing about. He didn't want any part of it. He was a businessman. The South was his home, not Nasir's.

Nasir's noticed Fulton's hesitation. "You fuckin' coming?" he shouted.

Fulton sighed heavily and climbed into his Jaguar. He felt less confident than Nasir, even though he was carrying his Ruger SR9. His boy got into the passenger seat. Fulton reluctantly led the way to the trailer park in the hood. Spartanburg was known to be a very violent county—

niggas there really didn't give a fuck about life or death. A lot of killers were bred in Spartanburg, and they didn't like niggas from Greenville. Fulton took a deep breath and navigated his car out of the parking lot and headed toward the sprawling trailer park in Roebuck.

"I hope this muthafucka don't get us killed tonight," Fulton said to his boy.

His boy remained quiet—stoic.

Fulton led the way, traveling on John B. White Blvd. It was late, and there was no traffic; most everything was closed and there was no sign of life.

Nasir followed closely behind Fulton. They traveled down 295 into Roebuck and came into the expansive trailer park known as Oakwood Homes. The area was poor and rundown with residents that were stereotypically viewed as white trash or trailer-park trash. The majority of the occupants were living below the poverty line, having a low social status and leading a haphazard and toxic lifestyle.

The rural area was covered with dilapidated trailer homes sitting on cinder blocks not secured to the ground. Trash was scattered everywhere, uncut weeds and dead grass inundating the area, and a few old junk cars were parked in every driveway. It was the epitome of poor. Chained and loose dogs barked loudly seeing the sudden presence of the unwanted company, and residents passed time by drinking and gambling.

Fulton's Jaguar and Nasir's burgundy Cadillac lights were turned off and they slowly looked for the address that was given to Fulton by a close associate. They soon found it. Fulton stopped his ride, not proceeding any farther. Nasir stopped behind him. The men exited their cars. Nasir looked angrily at the badly maintained trailer home. He noticed the black Yukon, parked slightly out of sight next to it. It screamed a heavy drug dealer's car with the 24-inch chromed rims and blacked-out headlights. It had to be Demon's car, which stood out in the area like a chess piece on a checkerboard. It didn't belong. Finally, Nasir would come face-to-face with the man the South had been living in fear of.

"What now?" Fulton asked.

There was no "what now" for Nasir. He opened the trunk of the Cadillac and removed a baseball bat and another automatic pistol. The "what now" was doing the inevitable. The "what now" was killing Demon and everyone inside.

Nasir shut the trunk, and with the metal baseball bat gripped tightly in one hand and the .9mm in the other, he methodically approached the trailer home. Fulton pulled out his Ruger and his boy gripped a .45. They followed behind Nasir toward the trailer with some acquiescence.

There were a few lights on in the trailer home. It was too risky to just charge inside, so Nasir came up with a simple game plan: Have them come outside into an ambush. He looked at Fulton for a moment. "Be ready," he said, self-assured.

Fulton and his boy nodded.

Nasir raised the baseball bat and took a powerful swing at the lavish Yukon, smashing in the windows and triggering the loud alarm. It blared. Nasir pivoted toward the trailer entrance, and with his arm outstretched, aimed his pistol at the doorway waiting for the first victim to come charging out. Fulton and his friend did the same. It didn't take long for the front to fly open, and a shirtless male came hurrying outside. There was no hesitation; Nasir opened fire.

Bak! Bak! Bak!

The shirtless male went down swiftly, crumpling down on the stairway with three shots in his chest. Fulton shouted, "That's not Demon! That's not him!"

Nasir rushed toward the trailer. He was adamant to end this manhunt tonight. When he got to the doorway, shots were fired back at him. He ducked as bullets lodged in the doorframe, missing him, and he returned fire. A woman started yelling frantically, then a child started to cry.

"Fuck y'all! You come to my fuckin' home! I'll kill you, muthafuckas!" a man inside the trailer shouted heatedly. "Fuck you! You know who the fuck I am!! I'm Demon! I can't die, muthafuckas!!"

Boom! Boom! Boom!

Everything was moving in a blur. More gunfire between the men ensued. Nasir crouched low and rushed into the trailer with his gun in front of him and caught a glimpse of Demon escaping out the back door. There was a dark-skinned young woman with long microbraids clad in a long T-shirt on the floor, clutching her crying daughter to her chest. Her face was flooded with tears. She glared at Nasir and screamed, "Leave us alone! Get the fuck outta my house!"

Fortunately for the woman, Nasir went chasing after Demon, leaving the her hollering in her home. He hurried out the back door and ran into the darkened woods. He could see a figure sprinting ahead of him. He shot at the shadowy silhouette incessantly but missed. He ran deeper into the woods, with nothing but a little bit of light from the full moon above to illuminate the night. He zeroed in on his target and fired again, but missed a second time. Moving through the thick trees and wild shrubbery like lightening, he stumbled somewhat over branches and rocks, almost falling flat on his face, but he quickly regained his footing and continued. He didn't know the woods, so he had to be extra careful.

Suddenly, gunfire was heard from a distance and bullets went whizzing by his ear. Now it felt like he was becoming the hunted. Nasir stopped, finding himself in the middle of nowhere. He rapidly scanned the area around him. His heart was beating a thousand times per minute. He was winded and angry. He had lost Demon.

"Fuck!" he shouted with rage.

Nasir's eyes zigzagged everywhere. He gritted his teeth with his nostrils flaring. He told himself to think—don't panic. He continued to take in his surroundings and immediately saw an obscure figure charging at him. The night lit up with rapid gunfire and Nasir ducked, taking cover in the grassy field behind a large tree. He could hear the bullets tearing into the bark.

"You come fo' me, muthafucka? You put my family in danger? I'm personally gonna shoot both yo' fuckin' eyes out!" Demon screamed madly. "This is my home, muthafucka! I'ma send you back to New York in pieces!"

Boom! Boom! Boom! Boom!

Nasir could feel the blast from the powerful gun Demon shot shredding the tree apart. He was rushing closer. Nasir gripped his handgun and took a deep breath. He didn't come this far to die in South Carolina. He thought about Red and scowled heavily. Demon was almost up on him, the gunfire splintering the tree he hid behind.

"I'ma fuck you up, nigga! I'ma fuck you up!" Demon screamed.

He continued to fire.

Boom! Boom . . . click, click . . .

Nasir was far too familiar with that sound. The gun was empty—stupid muthafucka. It was an unfortunate blunder for Demon. Nasir removed himself from his hiding position and fixed his glare on Demon. He had his arm outstretched with the pistol at the end of it. The two men gazed at each other briefly. Demon didn't flinch or seem intimidated by the hostile position he suddenly found himself in. He remained deadpan and undaunted.

Demon was a massive looking man with thick, twisting dreadlocks and a thick beard. He stood six-three and was physically fit with muscles. His eyes were cold toward Nasir. The huge, empty gun still remained in his hand. He looked like pure evil.

Demon smirked and commented harshly, "What the fuck you gon' do wit' that, muthafucka?"

"My job," Nasir replied matter-of-factly.

Nasir was no fool. The man could easily break him in half and snap his neck like he was a twig. He could see why the South feared him. But Nasir wasn't from the South, and Demon didn't put fear in his heart either. No matter how big or tall the nigga was, he was still a man and could bleed easily like everyone else. Nasir had the advantage.

"This ain't even about the missing five kilos anymore," said Nasir through clenched teeth. "This shit is personal."

"Fuck you and yo' friend! Fuck y'all New York niggas!" Demon hollered.

Bak! Bak! Bak!

Nasir quickly put three shots into Demon's chest, causing him to jerk backwards from the impact. Surprisingly, he didn't fall or collapse. Demon was shocked, but he still stood tall, grasped his wounds, and glared at Nasir. He was stunned. Demon slowly approached Nasir, and he fired again, and this time Demon stumbled and dropped on one knee. He couldn't be Superman forever—bullets hurt, and eventually, they killed. Demon started to choke on his own blood. Nasir moved in closer for the kill. This time, it was Nasir towering over Demon as the man was on his knees, severely injured and propped against a tree. Nasir put the pistol to Demon's forehead and didn't hesitate. He fired the final round into his head, and Demon tumbled over on his side.

Nasir pumped four more rounds into his lifeless frame. It was finally over with. He left the body to rot and the animals to tear it apart.

When he got back to the trailer park, there were police lights everywhere. He couldn't go back the way he'd come, so he had to turn around and trek back into the woods for a half-hour until he came across a paved road and some cell-phone service. It was a daunting hike. Once back into civilization, he called Fulton to pick him up.

The following day, Nasir was packed and ready to go. Five days spent away from New York and his business up north was too long of a time. He wanted to leave before police started coming around asking questions. Too many people had seen his face. Word had quickly gotten around about Demon's death, and while the majority were elated to hear about his demise, there were a few who wanted revenge. Nasir wasn't going to stick around to confront any retribution against him.

Before he got on the 1-85 back to New York, he put a bullet into Fulton's head and stuffed him into the trunk of his Jaguar. Nasir was tired of him. He felt that Fulton was too weak and he didn't trust him at all. He left the responsibilities of distributing drugs in the South to Fulton's right-hand man, Chance.

The South was hell for Nasir, and he had a bone to pick with Fancy once he arrived back in New York.

CHAPTER 12

Fancy and Pippa shared a refined glass of white wine by the pool of her Long Island estate. It was a beautiful Sunday evening, and the two talked and socialized like they were old friends having drinks. It had been almost a week since their meeting at club Oasis, and the background on Pippa came back a sure thing. She was who she said she was in Miami, and the information from her peoples appeased Fancy. Fancy had a new connection in Miami that seemed profitable. But the problem was, she wondered if she'd step on any toes by dealing with Pippa from Miami. Miami was a huge and profitable playground, and greed was talking over more than her common sense.

Clad in a crochet net cover-up dress with her bikini underneath, Fancy sat in the poolside chair with her legs crossed and talked details with Pippa about prices and distribution into the sunshine state.

"I can go as low as seventeen thousand a ki," Fancy said to Pippa.

"Seventeen, I probably can do seventeen . . . and what about delivery?"

"I have a team of union workers and legit drivers moving product for me through a secured pipeline on the interstates. I will not go into details about it, but with the money I'm paying for protection and transportation, I haven't had any problems yet. " Fancy said. "I plan on keeping it that way."

Pippa nodded. Fancy had her organization well put together in a few months' time. With the cartel backing her, Fancy's power and reach seemed endless.

The two were becoming friends in a very short time, but they were still getting to know each other. Fancy took a sip of wine and eyed Pippa slyly from head to toe. She was extremely beautiful. The yellow and turquoise paisley bikini Pippa wore showed off her curves, ass, tits and sexiness in so many ways. Fancy convinced herself that she wasn't attracted to Pippa—that she wasn't a lesbian, but there was something about her that was so enticing.

"You are so beautiful," Fancy found herself saying out of the blue.

Pippa smiled and replied with, "Thank you. And so are you."

"So enough business for today. Tell me a little more about yourself, Pippa."

Pippa reclined in the poolside chair and sipped on the fine wine. Her composure was too cool. After tasting the wine, she pulled out a cigarette and lit up. She took a few strong pulls, exhaled, and gazed at Fancy like she had much admiration for the young girl.

"I respect you, Fancy," Pippa started.

Fancy was flattered by the comment, but it wasn't what she had asked Pippa.

Pippa took a few more pulls of smoke and continued with, "To be honest with you, I love pussy. I love women."

Fancy wasn't shocked by her comment. She remained quiet.

"I know when we first met, you said you didn't swing that way, but have you ever been with a woman or thought about being with a woman?"

"I'm strictly dickly," replied Fancy. "No offense."

Pippa smiled. "None taken. But it's what we all say sometimes, until that right woman comes into your life and influences you to rethink your sexuality. I'm very comfortable with mine, are you?"

"Oh, I'm very comfortable with mine, Pippa," Fancy replied assuredly with direct eye contact.

"You have a man in your life?"

"I do."

"You love him?"

"It's none of your business," Fancy replied sternly.

"It's okay. I'm not trying to intrude into your personal life."

Pippa was clearly much older than Fancy and more experienced—also manipulative and cunning. She had seen woman like Fancy come and go all her life. Fancy had the power and upper hand today, but things always changed in Pippa's favor tomorrow. Fancy may have proclaimed to love dick and her man, but once Pippa was done with her and turned her out, the fun would truly begin, and the revenge was going to be so sweet.

"You find me attractive, Fancy?" Pippa asked facetiously.

"I'm not going to lie to you, but I do find you very attractive," Fancy replied. "But I'm no dyke and I don't mix business with pleasure."

That what they all say, Pippa thought to herself. But she came back with, "There's no need to. And I respect that."

Pippa crossed her legs slowly in front of Fancy. They were so smooth and milky-looking. Fancy and Pippa continued talking while relaxing by the pool on a hot, sunny evening. It was an unruffled moment, with their wild lives put on hold for the evening.

Fancy engaged her time heavily with Pippa until she noticed Nasir walking out onto the deck of their home. She turned to gaze at her lover, and so did Pippa. The look Nasir had was sour. He scowled and was silent for a moment. Fancy was aware that things hadn't gone as smoothly as planned in South Carolina. Pippa gazed at him too, assuming he was Fancy's man.

Nasir cut his eyes over at Pippa and walked toward the two women seated by the poolside with an angry stride. He didn't like what he was seeing at all. Who was this new bitch in Fancy's life? And why was she at their home? He was truly irked by her presence, among other things, too.

"Nasir," Fancy called out. "Hey baby."

She stood to her feet. Pippa remained seated, keeping her cool. It was evident that the man was upset about something.

"Who the fuck is this bitch and why is she in our fuckin' crib?" Nasir bluntly and rudely exclaimed.

"Nasir, be nice. She's my guest," Fancy spat back.

"Your guest?"

"Yes!"

Nasir cut his eyes over at Pippa. He immediately didn't like her. Pippa stood to her feet, smiling while oozing sexiness in front of Nasir and not becoming offending by his harsh remarks. She read him at once—bad boy, killer, and a very dangerous man.

"So, you're Nasir. It's finally nice to meet you," Pippa greeted, extending her hand to him.

Nasir looked at her coldly, ignoring her friendly gesture.

"Get a clue, bitch. I'm not in the mood to be fuckin' socializing!" he barked.

"Well Fancy is . . ."

Nasir cut his eyes back toward Fancy. She was frowning—seething from his out-and-out disrespect to a guest in her home. Nasir didn't want to be bothered. He'd had a very long drive from South Carolina, and Red was dead. Also, Nasir didn't take too lightly to new faces and strangers. He felt that having her in their Long Island estate, where they lay their heads could turn out to be a grave mistake. That was rule number one in the hustling handbook.

"I need to talk to you," Nasir said with a grimace toward Fancy.

"You don't run a damn thing in this house, Nasir!"

"Maybe I fuckin' need to, cuz you ain't fit to run shit, Fancy!"

"Fuck you, Nasir!"

"No, fuck you, bitch!"

Pippa stood closely to the feuding couple. Hearing them argue like that was music to her ears. She kept her composure and feigned some concern toward their dispute.

"Fancy, I'm okay, go talk to your man and I'll just leave," Pippa said sincerely.

"Good idea!" Nasir agreed.

"You don't have to go anywhere, Pippa. Stay! You're my company, not his. I run things around here," Fancy said, grandstanding.

"We really need to talk, Fancy!" Nasir exclaimed.

"And we will, on my fuckin' time, Nasir, not yours!" screamed Fancy. Nasir glared at her with a look to kill.

Fancy continued with, "Now you either apologize to Pippa or you can leave, and I'll deal with you later," Fancy said dismissively.

"Deal with me?" Nasir was incredulous. It was clear that the spoiled, stuck up brat bitch was back. The same girl he'd met a couple years back when she came to his mother's doorstep, broke and destitute. Fancy was speaking to Nasir as she had spoken to her maid or gardener in the past.

"Yes, deal with you!" Fancy warned heatedly.

"Red is dead because of you! We went down to South Carolina to handle business for you, and I come back home to this type of treatment? New fuckin' faces in our home and you being a dumb ass bitch!"

"Nasir, you're treading on thin ice. I warn you, shut your mouth before you say something that you're going to regret," Fancy said.

"I already said and did things I regret, but you, you're fuckin' slippin' Fancy," he shouted.

Fancy didn't scare Nasir. He didn't care what position she was placed in—he would always remember her as that scared, naive little girl moving into the hood for the first time because Mommy and Daddy got locked up. Now all of a sudden she wanted to stunt on him like she was a threat. Nasir didn't give a fuck. He still loved her, but the love seemed to only be going down a one-way street.

Fancy's eyes burned into Nasir. Pippa stood quietly in the background watching the fireworks going off. Everything was working out for her perfectly. After her fight with Nasir, Fancy would be looking for someone to confide in. It was natural with woman, and Pippa wanted to be that woman Fancy could lean on and talk about her problems to—and maybe reveal some useful information about her father, too.

Nasir was ready to turn away from Fancy and leave. She was becoming impossible to deal with. Power and wealth was going to her head, and she was becoming unreasonable. He was fuming because they both made it clear that no one, except for probably their close, immediate family—his mother and his siblings—were allowed into the home where they laid their heads every night. And after all they'd been through, Nasir assumed that Fancy would comprehend the meaning of keeping a low profile. Seeing Pippa in their home compromised everything and put their lives at risk. Nasir been in the streets long enough to understand that you keep a tight circle, trust no one, and absolutely never bring outsiders to your place of rest.

"Just get the fuck out my face, Nasir . . . leave me! Leave us!" Fancy exclaimed.

Nasir was ready to explode and beat the shit out of her, but he restrained himself, and not because of any cartel. She had his heart and he couldn't see laying hands on her.

Fancy added insult to injury when she said, "I don't need you, Nasir, you need me, so don't you ever fuckin' forget that."

Nasir could see Pippa smirking in the background. The vibes he got from her weren't good. There was something about her that he didn't like. It was too bad that Fancy didn't have that same instinct.

Nasir was tired of arguing with Fancy. She showed him who she was a long time ago.

It had been a stressful week with him almost losing his life twice and Red being killed. *No more,* he thought. He was a boss too, and he was tired of being treated like some lackey.

"Y'all bitches have fun wit' each other. And fuck you, bitch, I'm out!" said Nasir, turning away from both women and leaving abruptly.

Fancy grimaced heavily at his comment and wondered if she had taken shit too far. She thought Nasir understood her position and that she couldn't look weak in front of anyone. In life, everyone had a position to play. Her mother played her position while Alexandro perpetrated a fraud and represented himself to everyone as first in command. That had to have been hard for Belen. Yet she did it because she saw the bigger picture.

Why couldn't Nasir be more like Belen and see the bigger picture?

The bigger question was, if Nasir was Belen, would that make Fancy, Alexandro?.

Fancy fumed as she watched Nasir leave their estate.

"He's a charmer," Pippa joked.

Fancy turned and shot a torturous look at Pippa that said she wasn't in the mood to have her in her personal business.

"I'm sorry."

Fancy felt she didn't need anyone, especially not the past counsel from her mother and aunt, and any further protection from Nasir. She had too much to prove.

CHAPTER 13

"Fancy, I'm so fuckin' disappointed with you. What is wrong with you? You have to be the stupidest bitch out there!"

Belen's attitude was becoming very tiresome for Fancy. Her words were callous and disturbing. It seemed Belen was becoming more and more bitter toward her daughter with every visit.

Fancy glared at her mother, keeping her cool even when she had the strong urge to jump across the table and attack her in her seat. Fancy wasn't a scrapper, though. Probably couldn't win a fist fight with a twelve year old, but she knew how to pull out and use her heat, and at the moment she wanted to put two bullets in Belen's dome.

She thought her mother was upset with her about not paying Gary Scheck his $500,000 fee for her case. Or maybe Belen found out about the business arrangement she had with him. Either way, Fancy had other priorities to take care of rather than cater to Belen.

"I fuckin' warned you, Fancy, to keep quiet about everything I told you about Jesus," Belen spat with her face twisted and fist clenched.

Fancy was confused. "What are you talking about?"

"Who did you tell about him being your father?"

"I told no one! I didn't even tell Nasir," Fancy strongly let her mother know.

Belen shot a dubious stare at her daughter. "You're lying! Someone said something."

"I don't see what's the big deal is of keeping it a secret anyway," returned Fancy. "He is my father, right?"

Belen remained silent. Her anger for her daughter had turned into concern now. She sighed heavily, and for a split moment, she saw the little girl she raised when times were good and life seemed normal. But it had gotten back to Belen inside the prison that Jesus had another daughter, and the streets were talking heavily about it.

"He is."

"I'm his daughter. It couldn't be kept a secret for too long," said Fancy with a nonchalant tone.

"It needed to be kept a secret in order for you to stay alive, Fancy. You clearly do not understand the danger involved," Belen heatedly told her.

Fancy continued with her blasé demeanor. She had her power and goons, so if any danger came her way, then she was ready for it. But Belen couldn't keep her daughter in the dark any longer. The truth had to be revealed to her.

"Listen to me Fancy, and listen carefully. Your life is in danger."

"How?" asked Fancy.

Belen fixed her hard eyes on Fancy's angelic features and went on to say, "Late last year, word went around the prison system that Jesus' oldest child, Marisol, and her whole family was massacred in Colombia. The heads and hands of each victim were never found, but the DNA made a positive ID."

The news didn't frighten Fancy. She sat stoically and continued to listen. She really didn't give a fuck. But there was much more for Belen to tell her.

Belen leaned closer to her daughter. "And his middle daughter, Maribel and her whole family of six disappeared around the same time

131

and no bodies have been found yet. It's real out there, Fancy, and you have no idea what these people are capable of doing. They are sadistic."

Fancy didn't understand what her mother was telling her and why it had anything to do with her. The lackadaisical response Fancy kept feeding back to her made Belen shake her head in disgust.

"If someone is out there killing Jesus' kids, you could be next, Fancy."

Fancy still wasn't worried. Her reply was, "You obviously don't understand my status in this game. I'm a boss bitch now, and I can handle myself. And I'm in America; this isn't Colombia." The coldness of her tone exemplified the heartless bitch she'd become.

"You're a damn fool, Fancy," Belen retorted.

"I'm not a little girl anymore, Mother. I would say you taught me well growing up, but you ain't teach me shit."

It was time for her to leave. She was done with the visit. She stood up, indicating her departure to the guards, and walked away leaving her mother fuming at her ignorance.

❦

Nasir sat behind the wheel of his Benz under the fading sun in the heart of Brooklyn—Brownsville—out here, niggas never hide. Rockaway Avenue was packed with people, traffic, beat cops, and trouble. The bustling, concrete jungle was noisy, stinking, and turbulent, but it would always be home to him. After experiencing the South for almost a week, there was no place like home. He smoked a Newport and gazed out the window, staring at his young niggas working the block fervently.

With a lot on his mind, Nasir felt trapped in a closing environment that was trying to swallow him up whole. Pippa was becoming a regular face around Fancy and the organization, and it was not only irking him, but also troubling. She had Fancy ready to set up shop in Miami. Even though Fancy was a queen-pin, she was still a rookie to the major players of the underworld, and Nasir didn't like that arrangement. Miami was too close to the Colombians, the Cubans, the Haitians, and so many other notorious figures, and he didn't want any part of that place. But greed and lack of common sense was gripping Fancy—or sinking her like quicksand— and it was becoming a headache to deal with. He wondered how Pippa had so much influence on the woman he supposedly loved. Fancy was smart, yes, but she had her flaws, too, and he felt bringing that bitch Pippa into their world would cost them, maybe even fatally. He decided to do a background check of her on his own. There was just something about her that he didn't like and certainly didn't trust.

Jo-Jo and Pete stood in front of the neglected Chinese food store looking harrowing and mean. They were notorious on the streets. The two lads were Nasir's young goons and killers who took orders from him without questions.

Nasir flicked his cigarette out the window and stepped out his car. He easily approached Jo-Jo and Pete with an unsmiling expression. The word was out; Nasir was the number two man in charge of a violent drug empire pushing the most potent product on the streets right now, and he had the blessing of the cartel. He was a scary guy to everyone.

He walked up to Jo-Jo and Pete and greeted them with a fist pound and respect. The two killers always became submissive in front of their boss.

"Y'all niggas good?" Nasir asked.

"Yeah, we right, Nasir. You got some work fo' us?" asked Pete.

"Yeah, I might."

Pete nodded. His look was menacing with his large facial scar and beady eyes, and he was always whistling, especially when it came time to put in some work.

"We bored right now, Nasir," said Pete.

"Any luck on finding Li'l-Un?" Nasir asked.

"He still ghost. I mean, we been askin' around and shit, but the nigga ain't been seen in the hood in almost four months," Jo-Jo stated.

Nasir was still itching to find the muthafucka and deal with him.

The block was flooded with locals moving about on a sunny evening. Some faces he knew and many he didn't. While lingering on the corner with Jo-Jo and Pete, a dark-colored Denali came to a stop at a red light at the corner and the occupants inside stared strongly at Nasir and his thugs. The driver especially scowled heavily at the dwellers on the Brooklyn corner. He focused on Nasir. His intense look was highly threatening. Nasir scowled back and was preparing for a confrontation.

The nippy standoff was fleeting. Nasir didn't recognize any of their faces, but they looked hardcore enough to shoot up a public block. He didn't underestimate anyone in this line of business. When the light changed green, the Denali slowly drove away, leaving Nasir cautious of the vehicle.

"Who the fuck are them niggas?" he asked Jo-Jo and Pete.

"Don't know. They been driving by here mean-mugging muthafuckas for the past three weeks now. They ain't leap yet. But I tell you what, if they rise up, they gon' get laid the fuck down," Pete said with certainty.

Something was wrong, and Nasir had a gut feeling it was only the beginning of something dreadful. Maybe it was a rival crew trying to muscle in on new territory, or someone connected to the Colombians checking up on them—he even came up with the absurd thought that Fancy sent goons of her own into his hood to keep an eye out for him. It was a thin line between love and hate—trust and deceit.

No longer feeling comfortable on the street corner, Nasir said goodbye to his men and climbed back into his Benz. He observed his surroundings extra carefully and decided it was best to lie low for a minute. But if shit jumped off, then he was ready.

He pulled away from the curb and headed toward the freeway located a few miles down the road. But the minute he left the area, he noticed that he was being tailed.

"What the fuck!" He eyed the black sedan in his rearview mirror.

He pulled out the .44 Magnum wedged in his seat and placed it on his lap. He drove slowly through the confined, city streets. He continuously shifted his attention from the road to the car following behind him. When he came close to the Belt Parkway, the sedan approached him more closely.

"Muthafuckas wanna follow me…a'ight," Nasir said to himself.

He came to a stop at a red light. He was ready to gun through the light and make a break for the highway. But the traffic in front of him was thick. He could only wait, idling at the intersection and becoming vigilant of everything with his hand gripped around the .44.

The light changed to green, and he sped off, but instantly the blue lights glaring behind him indicated police presence.

"Fuck!" Nasir cursed.

It was police following him the entire time. He hadn't committed any traffic infractions and maintained the speed limit. The problem was that it was an unmarked car, and usually when an unmarked followed you for blocks and suddenly pulled you over, they weren't giving out traffic tickets.

Nasir immediately placed the .44 Magnum into a hidden compartment and kept his cool. Besides the gun, his ride was clean and the car was legit. Two tall white men exited the sedan—detectives, and slowly approached the Benz. They were in street attire with their badges and holstered guns placed on their hips. Nasir recognized one of them immediately. He sighed with reluctance and knew this wasn't a social stop.

Nasir kept cool. They approached both sides of the car; the detective Nasir was familiar with came toward the driver-side window.

"Nasir, Nasir, Nasir, it's good to finally see you again. It's been a minute," the detective said contemptuously.

"Detective Cooper, why this stop?" Nasir asked calmly .

"This is a really nice car," Cooper said.

"Yeah . . . thanks," Nasir replied dryly.

"But I just wanted to reacquaint myself with you. This is my new partner, Zane," said Cooper.

Nasir wasn't interesting in any small talk with the detectives. He remained aloof, looking away from both detectives that flanked his pricey Benz. It was a procedure from the police that he was used to enduring. Cooper, with his-salt-and pepper goatee and short-cropped hair, was a veteran detective from the 79th Precinct, and Nasir had been on his shit list of prominent arrest for several years now, but the adept drug dealer was always able to evade capture.

"I'm hearing big things about you, Nas. The streets are saying you came up, that you're no longer a punk, gun-toting corner drug dealer anymore. I haven't seen you around the way lately, so the rumors about you must be true, although I say differently. You're still a young, dumb punk in my eyes," said Cooper with an intense glare.

"I'm a businessman now, Detective Cooper," Nasir replied nonchalantly.

Cooper chuckled. "Businessman, now that's hilarious. You're a murderous thug, Nasir, a cold-hearted killer that will soon have his end of days and receive life in prison like they all do. I promise you that."

"So you say."

"So I say, huh. You're funny, but I'm gonna need for you to step out of the car please," Cooper requested.

Nasir was hesitant, but he was in no position to protest. He grimaced. He had important things to do.

Cooper sternly said, "I'm not gonna ask again."

Nasir swung open the car door and jumped out. He was immediately thrown against the car with his hands on the hood. Detective Cooper patted him down while detective Zane rummaged through the vehicle searching for any contraband or weapons.

"This is what you call police harassment and my lawyer is gonna have a field day wit' y'all," Nasir griped.

"Tell him to get in line, muthafucka, because we don't give a fuck!" Cooper retorted.

Nasir felt violated as Cooper thoroughly patted him down, going through each of his pockets and making him take off his shoes and belt. Nasir scowled. He so badly wanted to take a swing at the detective and knock out every tooth, but he had to hold his composure.

Cooper roughly threw Nasir against the hood of the car repeatedly, catching the attention of several passersby in their cars witnessing the police harassment in public view. But no one dared to intervene. Their curiosity was brief, and they kept on to their own destinations.

Cooper glared at Nasir and said, "We know about Shoe-Shine, Nasir. That boy was found along with your drug connect, Tone, shot to death in a darkened alley. He's was your boy, Nasir, and you had your partner in crime murdered. We can't link you to the homicides just yet, but we will. We have witnesses."

Nasir looked indifferent. They didn't have any witnesses, and he wasn't the one who killed Shoe-Shine. It was Fancy, so he didn't break a sweat about the incident.

"Witnesses," he laughed. "How you gonna have witnesses to a crime that I didn't even commit? Shoe-Shine knew the game, we all do. That was my dude, but life goes on."

Cooper wanted to bang Nasir's head against the concrete. His hatred for the violent young drug dealer was visible through every square, Caucasian inch of him. There wouldn't be anything better for him to see than Nasir either receiving life in prison or the death penalty.

Nasir showed off a smug look. They had nothing on him. Everything was all a bluff. He was on top. Nasir chuckled. The smug look infuriated detective Cooper to the breaking point where he punched Nasir in the face and almost sent the young hood flying across the hood of his Benz. The blow was stunning; Nasir was caught off guard by the hit, and even detective Zane was surprised by the sudden attack.

"Cooper, what is wrong with you?" Zane shouted, and halted his search of the vehicle.

"Fuck him!" Cooper screamed out.

Nasir had blood trickling from the corner of his mouth. He was fuming. No one ever disrespected him like that. Ever. He glared at the detective, wiped the blood from his mouth, and uttered, "You're a dead man, Detective."

"Am I? Are you threatening a cop now?" Detective Cooper exclaimed.

"That's exactly what I'm doin'," Nasir chided.

"Oh, so you just threatened me. You're now under arrest for threatening and insulting a police officer," Cooper exclaimed.

He grabbed Nasir roughly and spun him around, slamming him against the hood of his car, bending his arms behind him and quickly placing the handcuffs around his wrists.

"I'll be out in a fuckin' hour," Nasir growled with conviction.

"We'll see about that, muthafucka."

Nasir was thrown into the back of the unmarked car. Detective Cooper had had a hard-on for Nasir since he shot and killed one of Cooper's close informants several years ago and was acquitted of the murder because of witness intimidation and lack of evidence.

For one last blatant fuck-you to Nasir, Cooper smashed in the back window to his new C63 AMG Benz.

Cooper and his partner climbed into the car. He turned around with his smug grin and said to Nasir, "You may be out in twenty-four hours, muthafucka, but for the next twenty-four hours, you're fuckin' mine."

Nasir remained cold .

"Whatever, bitch," Nasir refuted.

The detective drove away, heading in a different direction from the precinct. Nasir knew what was coming next for him. Cooper did things his own way and played by his own set of rules, sometimes dishing out his own form of street justice when the real justice system didn't work in his favor.

"Yeah, not so tough now, huh, Nasir?" Cooper taunted.

Nasir frowned and remained silent. He just wanted to get it over with.

CHAPTER 14

Nasir pulled up to the sprawling, Long Island estate in the late evening in yet another sour mood. His torturous moment with detective Cooper left a bad taste in his mouth, and a few bruises. Nasir didn't step foot into any precinct, but received his punishment on the hard end of a steel baton that came down across his body repeatedly. The blows from the baton almost broke a few of his ribs. Cooper was a borderline dirty and racist cop who wasn't going to rest until Nasir was either locked up or dead.

He was ready to green-light a hit on the detective, and he planned on using the cartel to do his dirty work. The disrespect shown to him over the past twenty-four hours was humiliating and awkward, and he had had enough of the harassment.

Nasir walked into the home he shared with Fancy with a burning desire to destroy something. The place was quiet. He placed his guns on the table and wanted to change into something more decent. His shirt was torn and had sprinkles of blood on it, and his side was aching. He refused to go to any hospital and receive medical treatment. The last thing he wanted to do was bring on any attention upon himself. And he wasn't a snitch, even if it was a cop that did him wrong and beat the shit out of him.

Nasir went up the spiral stairway and walked into the master bedroom. He heard the shower running in the next room. Assuming Fancy was taking a shower; he started to undress and had the urge to join her in the steamed shower. He needed to soothe the aching in his bones. Shirtless and tending to his soreness by massaging his bruises and looking in the mirror, he was taken aback by noticing Pippa standing in the doorway to the bedroom. She was completely naked, and also pretended to be startled at the sight of Nasir. But soon the forced shock on her face turned into a flirtatious smile.

"What the fuck are you doing here?" Nasir exclaimed with his attention fixed on her nudeness.

"I was invited," she said with a teasing smile. "You okay?"

"I'm fine." He was short with her.

"I was just asking. You look hurt."

The sight of Pippa standing in the nude in front of him, made Nasir frozen with awe. She was extremely sexy. Pippa's beautiful face was surrounded by straight, but still beautiful, shiny raven-black tresses. Her hair flowed freely and framed her face and head perfectly. Her breasts with her chocolate-covered nipples could never be described as too large or too small—just perfect. Her curves and trim waist were appealing to any man's eyes and her shaven pussy was enticing. Nasir couldn't turn away from her. Her smile and beauty was tantalizing.

"You like what you see?" she asked seductively.

Nasir remained quiet. He could feel an erection growing in his jeans. He did like what he saw. She was tempting. Pippa stepped farther into the bedroom with her fervent gaze fixed on Nasir muscular physique. She knew he found her attractive. What man didn't? She thought the same of him; his smooth skin, dark shiny hair, bright white teeth, and mixed racial features were intoxicating.

"I can tend to your wounds. Let me help you," she said.

141

She stepped forward, grasping for his side. Nasir stepped away from her. She was a temptress. And daring. With Fancy in the shower in the other room, it was a stupid risk. Then Nasir had a deviant thought. He scowled and irritably asked, "Did you fuck her?"

Pippa smiled. "You want that?"

She slowly penetrated herself with two of her fingers and started to masturbate with Nasir as her witness. Nasir could only stare in wonderment. He was still a man. And his estranged relationship with Fancy wasn't making the situation any easier for him. He loved pussy. But there was something about her that he just didn't like.

Pippa continued to play with her pussy. She stared at Nasir, moaning from her own gratifying strokes and said, "You could fuck me. I won't tell."

It took all of Nasir's strength and will power not throw Pippa up against the wall and fuck her hard and obsessively.

He went toward Pippa with a change of mind and forcefully grabbed her by her arm and shoved her out the bedroom, exclaiming, "Get the fuck outta here! I don't need you. We don't fuckin' need you!"

He slammed the door in her face.

Pippa scowled, she wasn't used to being turned down. But she didn't become upset. It would only be a matter of time before she had them both wrapped around her finger and would have her way with them. Nasir couldn't resist her for too long. She noticed the way he looked at her.

Nasir sighed heavily. It had been a crazy week for him. He needed to do something to get his mind off the stress that he was dealing with. He removed the rest of his clothing and decided to join Fancy in the shower. He strutted into the tasteful bathroom with his dick swinging. He saw Fancy's sexy silhouette behind the glass shower door. The image was enticing, and with Pippa's naked body and her naughty exploit entrenched into his mind, he had one agenda—pussy.

Nasir threw back the glass, shower door and slipped into the steaming shower with Fancy. She had her eyes closed. Nasir reached around her waist and pulled her into his grasp, indicating his impulsive need for her. Fancy gasped, somewhat shocked by Nasir's unexpected presence. He made it clearly known what he wanted from her when he cupped her tits and began fondling her ass.

"Nasir, please . . . don't," Fancy started to say, showing some reluctance in giving him some pussy.

But Nasir wasn't taking no for an answer. He reached between her legs and started to fondle the delicate folds of her pussy, fingering her crimson inner lips, and toying with her dark nipples. He pinched them gently. He fingered her clit. Fancy wanted to resist him, but his touch was too soothing and good. Her slippery-sweet juices started to flow like wine becoming aroused by Nasir's erotic touch and feeling his throbbing, hard, big dick pressed against her ass. He kissed her body fervently and uttered in her ear, "I wanna fuck you."

Fancy became really aroused. Her clit was swollen and peeking out at Nasir, calling out for him. He took his index finger and rubbed it softly, making Fancy wiggle from the stimulating touch.

Fancy felt her legs opening up for his penetration. Nasir curved her over underneath the pouring shower and positioned his throbbing, hard dick near her goodies. Fancy placed both hands against the wall and arched her frame for easy entry into her pulsating womanhood. Their bodies needed it. She closed her eyes and waited for his dick to slide inside her. Nasir gripped her hips and thrust. He pumped his length and thickness inside her, pleasuring her punani. He drove in deeper and harder, causing Fancy to cry out in ecstasy.

Fucking her from the back, in the doggy-style position, ramming and plummeting his dick inside her with her juices seeping out on his shaft made Fancy lose control. Her breathing was erratic and out of control.

"Fuck me!" she cried out.

Nasir grunted and pushed inside of her. He pulled her closer, driving himself into her deeper and harder, and needing Fancy to cum as he navigated his own orgasm to time it with hers. Their bodies collided with an erotic purpose underneath the cascading showerhead. Fancy's moans grew louder and more urgent as she was coming to the brink of cumming. Being inside her gave him a temporary release with her legs trembling and hearing her muffled cries as her body tensed up.

Both their orgasms were heavy and intoxicating, as juices poured from each other causing a euphoric feeling that intensified, ending with tender kissing. .

Fancy stepped out of the shower and toweled off. Nasir lingered a little longer in the shower and soothed his bruises. She didn't even notice. Stepping out of the tub, he looked at Fancy tending to her long, wet hair in the mirror and the first words out of his mouth was, "Why is that bitch in this house?"

Fancy resented his statement. She turned and glared at Nasir and spat back, "This is my home, and I can have anyone I want here."

"This is my fuckin' home, too, Fancy, and I don't feel comfortable having that bitch around."

"You fuckin' jealous of her?" asked Fancy in a discourteous tone.

"You don't even know this bitch, and she always around. It's a stupid mistake."

"The way you're acting, I hardly know you now," she countered.

"After everything we fuckin' been through together, you start to doubt me and trust this bitch, Pippa?"

"I never said I trusted her."

"So who do you trust? Do you trust me?" Nasir asked.

Fancy remained silent. Her silence was her answer for Nasir.

"You don't trust me?"

KIM K.

Nasir wanted to tell her about the sexual advance Pippa made toward him earlier, but he decided to keep quiet about it. It seemed like the moment he started to talk about Pippa, Fancy would flip out and wanted to take his head off. The only thing he wanted to do was protect her and have her remain cautious about every little step she took. She not only endangered herself, but his well-being also.

Fancy stared at Nasir and honestly answered, "I don't know who to trust anymore."

"It's like that, huh?"

"I guess so."

Nasir couldn't believe what he just heard. He stormed out of the bathroom with the state of mind that if next time Pippa gave him the opportunity to fuck her again, he was going to take it. It seemed like Fancy was drifting from him, and he was becoming sick of her and her bossy attitude. He was a king, not someone's servant. And it was time she was remembered who the fuck he was and who taught who about the streets.

CHAPTER 15

It was Fancy's third meeting with Jesus in the posh penthouse suite in lower Manhattan, and she grew more and more comfortable with him each time she was in his presence. Dusk was over the city and a serene calm was felt in the room between Fancy and Jesus. She was hoping to bond more with her father.

He would summon Fancy, and she never hesitated to meet with him, even if it was only for an update on business. She suddenly found herself in his inner circle, whether it was inadvertently or not. Being around such a brooding and profound gangster who was adept with business and the underworld was an intimidating feeling. The power he had to crush or build someone or something made anyone tread lightly with either their words or their actions with him.

Jesus stood in front of Fancy clad in a black dress shirt, black slacks, and costly wingtips. His simple but expensive fashion sense manifested his introverted, but astute behavior.

"I see business is going really good for you. To us," Jesus said, raising his champagne to toast to her good fortune.

"Thanks to you, Mr. Negro," Fancy replied, raising her glass also.

They toasted, clinking glasses together.

He gazed at Fancy. Fancy had a lot on her mind, and she had the urge to confide in someone about her issues.

Jesus noticed the melancholic look on Fancy's face and he wanted to know the problem upsetting her. He downed his drink, stared at Fancy deeply, and said genuinely, "Tonight, your problems are my problems. I hate to see a beautiful woman upset when life should be blossoming for her."

Fancy could feel him soften up toward her. She didn't know what to say to him at first—issues from her mother, Nasir, and the game were becoming overwhelming sometimes, but she still held it all together.

Like a daughter confiding in her father, she said, "It's my boyfriend and my mother. I don't know what to do with them, Mr. Negro. They're both getting on my nerves. I think they're jealous of me. I'm constantly getting into arguments with the two people I love dearly in my life, and I can't understand why."

Jesus wanted to hear more about her mother, but before he could add his two cents, Fancy continued with, "I love Nasir, but he's changed since I started dealing with you."

"Sometimes men have a hard time dealing with women in authority," he replied cordially. "This Nasir, is he trustworthy?"

"I think so . . . yes," she replied lightly.

"Your hesitation shows your doubt for him. And your answer wasn't strong enough to be believable. Anyone so close to you, they must be trustworthy or why have them around? You have power now, Fancy. Do you know the true definition of power?"

She didn't reply.

"Power is having the ability to get results. Power is control, it's corrupting; it can stir jealousy in any subordinate beneath you . . . and it coming from a woman can cause most men to harbor deep resentment."

She thought about Nasir. Could he really accept her for the woman she had become? It had been easy for him to love her when he was the one pulling the strings and she was making out-of-state trips for him, becoming his mule and trafficking drugs. Or when she needed a place to stay and he was there for her, schooling and protecting her. He also took advantage of her and played her when she was a fledgling in his world. Now the shoe was on the other foot, and she had become the big bad wolf, and Nasir one of the three little pigs.

"This Nasir, he sounds like an interesting guy. I need to test him."

"Test him?"

"He's your boyfriend, and I would love to see if he truly has the stomach for what's to come in this business. And sometimes, there's more than one way to get your hands dirty besides being on the other end of a gun."

For a minute, Jesus sounded like a father who was ready to drill his daughter's boyfriend to make sure no harm came to her, and to assess if he was legit for her. The thought of it made Fancy want to smile. She missed it greatly with Alexandro.

"This Nasir, I want him to assist my men. I want to see the structure of this man."

Fancy nodded.

"And the issue with your mother?"

She was growing another headache.

"She has her case, this damn appeal, and they're transferring her to a different prison very soon . . . I think somewhere in Virginia or West Virginia. I don't care. She always expects me to do everything for her, and I can't be her keeper all the time."

"And how is she holding up?"

"My mother is a rock," Fancy replied.

Jesus remained deadpan. "You trust her, too?"

Fancy replied quickly, "She's my mother."

"Sometimes family can be the heart of the ultimate betrayal."

It made good sense, but Fancy knew Belen wasn't going to betray her.

The only thing Belen wanted to do was protect her.

"I understand," Fancy said.

Fancy wanted to reveal to him the things her mother told her, about both his children being murdered and mutilated in Colombia to see if it were true. She remembered the two names her mother told her: Maribel and Marisol. The information she received was ready to slip from her tongue, but she stopped herself. Fancy showed restraint. She was convinced that she was safe and in good hands. Nobody could touch her. But there was something sinister going on, which brought about an uneasy feeling in the pit of her stomach.

Jesus went on to give Fancy some fatherly advice about her situation. She listened intently, wanting nothing more than to please Jesus, her father on the down low. It was a good feeling for Fancy to chat with him in the privacy of his Manhattan suite. He seemed to have an open-door policy with her. But when would the time come when the cat was let out the bag, when she could call him her father and not have to worry about any repercussions?

Fancy and Pippa were having cocktails and brunch at Rue 57, a traditional European café uptown, across the street from Central Park. The area was abundant with affluent midtown residents of the neighborhood taking advantage of a beautiful summer day.

Fancy sipped on her latte while Pippa sunk her teeth into a delicious Greek salad. Fancy's henchmen were inconspicuously sitting at additional tables for her protection. The women received fleeting looks from the men in the area, but the ladies' standoffish attitudes kept them away.

Fancy had confided in Pippa about a few things, including the friction in her love life. Being a young woman and still a little green in many areas, she felt having a measure of girl talk with Pippa could do her some good. Maybe she could receive some sound advice about her turbulent relationship with Nasir. Pippa was older and seemed experienced in so many things, including love. Fancy respected the woman's intelligence and adventurous ways.

"He's jealous of you, Fancy. That's how I feel about it," said Pippa.

"Jealous?"

"Yes. Men like Nasir will never come to full terms with the fact that you're the one running things. You're a boss. His boss. Yeah, he'll tolerate it for a while, cuz you giving the nigga some pussy, making him feel really good. But he will always see you—us women—as inferior and weak. Especially since you succeeded in something he's been trying to attain his whole life: absolute power. It's like just because we have a pussy between our legs, not a fuckin' dick, we can't run an empire or be vicious like them, and we should spend our time on our knees or on our backs."

"I do love him," Fancy confessed.

"In our world, Fancy, love can get you killed. We don't have time for love. Love can make you look weak. And men like Nasir; they can be the cornerstone of your destruction. I've seen it so many times, even in my own life. I loved a man once, for five years, and he nearly destroyed me, my family, and everything I've built over the years because he couldn't handle my power or my authority and wanted to dominate me. It's the reason why I've turned to women and started chasing pussy. Men can be savages and tyrants, especially when it comes to the women in their lives. We can love a nigga really hard, but can they love us just as hard, without their egos and pride interfering?"

Fancy was absorbed by her words, listening intently.

Pippa continued with, "You and me, we are alike. We are survivors."

Fancy nodded. It was true. She thought about the day she was thrust into trying to survive after her parents' arrest. Everyone thought she was weak: it felt so good to prove them so wrong.

"We are," Fancy agreed.

"But remember you can't depend on no one, girl, in this business. Not even me. And I'm not saying I'm a snake bitch, but the wolves are around every corner," Pippa said sternly with her look glued to Fancy, who was almost young enough to be her daughter.

"Can I trust you, Pippa?" Fancy asked evenly.

Pippa stared at Fancy for a moment and casually responded with, "I think that's the stupidest question anyone could ever ask a person. Usually the reply is one of two answers: yes or no. And trust is never that black and white. It's grey. Dark grey—almost black, and definitely murky. If I said, you could trust me, would you? If I said, don't trust me, could you? My firm belief is that trust is something that's unobtainable, elusive. The very moment you decide to trust someone is that very moment you're fucked."

"So I'm fucked?"

"Are you?"

"I'm very simple, Pippa. You don't fuck with me and I don't fuck with you. That's my golden rule," Fancy returned with finality. She was tired of the riddles, fables, and the preachy sermon. The only person she respected to fill her mind with that type of wisdom was Alexandro. And Alexandro was dead.

"I guess it doesn't matter to you that I never answered your question. You've been such a gracious host, so I will humor you." Pippa took another sip of her Dirty Martini. "I do believe in fear, and as long as I fear you then I guess that will meet your interpretation of trust. So, to answer your question, Yes, you can trust me."

Fancy couldn't discern whether she was being mocked or praised, so she strategically decided to change course. "Damn, bitch, are you always this chatty and long winded when you get fucked up? If so, let this be ya last drink."

Pippa laughed, breaking the ice. "I will toast to that."

CHAPTER 16

"Por que Jesus nos han dando vueltas con los adolescents?" the Colombian thug uttered.

Nasir didn't understand one word he said, but he was familiar with the word "adolescents," and he could tell the four ominous-looking men in his presence were making fun of him in Spanish, which was disrespectful.

Nasir bellowed, "What the fuck you call me?"

"Amigo, relax. There's no need for the hostility. We are all the same," the passenger said with coolness. He was the alpha male of the group—the one in charge of the deed that had to get done.

"Fuck that, we ain't the same!" Nasir retorted.

"Tonight, Jesus want you to come, so you come," the man replied.

Nasir scowled. He had the urge to reply, "Fuck Jesus!" but he held his tongue. He was tired of taking orders from Fancy and now a foreigner.

Jesus reached out to him for a favor, if it was a favor. Nasir didn't really know what was up. He sat stone-faced and upset in the moving Tahoe going toward an unknown destination. Doing business with the cartel wasn't what he'd expected. He was reluctantly traveling with men he despised and knew nothing about. It was dusk out, cool, and becoming an uneasy night for him. Unexpectedly, the Colombians had come to his mother's place. Thinking that it was trouble or a setup, Nasir instantly reached for his pistol, but they came in peace and requested that he take a ride with them.

Nasir was reluctant. He didn't trust the Colombians at all and was highly suspicious of why they'd come for him. He tried asking questions, but they feigned ignorance and Nasir wasn't in any position to say he wasn't going.

Riding in the back and sandwiched between two towering thugs, Nasir felt vulnerable. They could be taking him to be slaughtered.

"Where we goin'?" Nasir asked.

"Like I said before, you ride and you see," the passenger said uncouthly.

The man was average height with dark, curly hair and a rough demeanor. His eyes were those of a coldhearted killer. Tonight, it felt like Nasir was about to become the victim, and he didn't know what he'd done wrong.

Did Fancy sanction a hit on him? Was she finally tired of arguing about Pippa? So many wild thoughts swam in his mind.

The truck drove north on I-87, going toward upstate New York. It was an intense, two-hour drive toward the men's destination, and once again Nasir found himself in the backwoods of Pennsylvania. The winding roads were pitch-black and too still. The driver stared down a dirt road and came upon a sprawling log cabin nestled behind towering trees and obscurity. It wasn't the same place he'd come to with Fancy.

The Tahoe came to a complete stop, and everyone exited the truck. Nasir was the last to get out. The men were speaking in Spanish, making Nasir feel like an outsider. He was the only black face in the dark.

Surrounded by miles of darkened woods and wild shrubbery, he had the urge to make a run for it. But where would he go? He was lost and miles away from Brooklyn. He wouldn't survive a day alone in the woods. He knew how to survive on the streets, but he didn't have a clue how to make it in the wilderness.

The superior of the group noticed Nasir's hesitation to enter the cabin. He stared at him and said, "C'mon, inside. We don't have time to waste."

"I ain't fuckin' goin' in there until I know what the fuck this shit is about," Nasir exclaimed.

"If you think we wanted to kill you, we could have already killed you in Brooklyn. You are one of us now, so you come, participate in our way," the man responded.

What way was that? Nasir wanted to know.

Nasir remained hesitant, but took the steps toward the cabin and walked inside behind the man. He didn't even know his name or the other three henchmen he was with. He took a deep breath and readied himself for the unpredictable.

Inside the barren cabin, there were two other armed Colombian goons waiting for their arrival and keeping watch over five men with hoods over their faces concealing their identities. The hooded men were all naked, beaten and frightened of the unknown, and they were also bonded with their hands behind their backs and on their knees.

Nasir gazed at the five poor souls in the room and felt relieved. This wasn't going to be his date of death. Nasir looked on with unconcerned eyes. He could give less than a fuck about their transgressions toward the cartel. They'd obviously fucked up and were about to pay the ultimate price for either their betrayal or rivalry.

He could hear them whimpering and begging for some kind of forgiveness under the stained hoods marked with the blood of previous victims.

One by one, their hoods were pulled from off their faces, revealing their identity. The captive men were of mixed races, three Colombians that had betrayed the cartel, one Hispanic that rivaled with the cartel, and one last man, yet to be revealed. There was some hesitation to remove the hood.

The superior stood in front of the last man. He then turned to look at Nasir for a moment. Nasir remained quiet. He could hear the man crying out, "Please . . . Please, I don't deserve this. I don't . . . please."

He snatched the hood from around the man's head and Nasir was stunned to finally see the identity of the man. It was one of his Brooklyn lieutenants, Jo-Jo.

"What the fuck!" Nasir shouted.

He rushed toward his homeboy and was ready to pull him out from the fire, but he was quickly restrained from doing so. The superior frowned at Nasir and said, "You're ready to jump into the fire and burn with this man when you haven't heard his crime yet."

"Let him go!" Nasir shouted.

"He betrayed you, Nasir."

"That's fuckin' bull-shit!" Nasir retorted.

"Where's Li'l-Un, Nasir?"

Hearing Li'l-Un's name coming from the Colombian's mouth made him cool down. Something was going on, and he was ready to hear some answers. "How do you know about him?"

"As your people would say, we keep our ears to the streets and know everything about everything. You are our investment. And we like to protect our investments."

Nasir was ready to listen to what he had to say.

He went on to say, "This man, the one you call Jo-Jo, was in cahoots with Li'l-Un to kill you and overtake your Brooklyn territory. We can't allow that to happen."

"Nasir, that's a fuckin' lie! I would never do you dirty! I got love for you, Nasir!" Jo-Jo cried out.

"Shut the fuck up!" Nasir screamed at him, blinded by rage.

He was ready to kill Jo-Jo himself.

"Where's Li'l-Un?" Nasir asked again.

"I don't know! I swear on my life!" Jo-Jo screamed. He was scared and just wanted to go home.

Nasir looked distastefully at Jo-Jo. Memories of being betrayed by Shoe-Shine came flooding back as he realized it was hard finding people you could trust when you're in the drug game.

The five naked men in the cabin knew of their fate. But unfortunately for them, the night had only just begun. And being in the middle of nowhere, their screams for mercy, forgiveness, and from the torture that was about to go down, wouldn't be heard at all—help was impossible for all five men.

The acting boss wanted to save the best for last. This was his forte. He was the number three man in Jesus' cartel. They called him Él Carnicero, which meant "the Butcher" in Spanish. His subordinate dropped a small bag filled with rusty, sharp tools near his feet. It was his kit of tools that had made some of the toughest men in the world scream and cry like babies.

He stared at his first victim intently. He wanted to make an example out of his own people first. Two men roughly pulled one naked man off his knees and strapped him to the wall with his arms outstretched toward the ceiling, iron bracelets clamped around his wrists. He was left vulnerable to be tortured.

"Lo siento, Carnicero . . . perdóname por favor! Por favor!" the man screamed frantically.

The methodical killer donned a black smock and thick goggles. Things were about to get really messy. Two knives were removed from the bag and he went straight for his ears and then the man's fingers were snapped off with sharp shears. Then he took a blowtorch to the prisoner's penis and scorched his private area until burning flesh reeked throughout the cabin.

What the fuck?! Nasir thought to himself. *This muthafucka sick.*

It was gory. There was blood and body parts everywhere, and it was only the beginning. Slowly, the victim was being ripped apart by sharp tools, looking like a jigsaw puzzle coming apart. Before the butcher moved on to his second victim, he placed a dagger to the man's neck and slowly carved his throat open.

The next three victims received the same horrid torture, repeatedly being stabbed, sliced, and cut open like fish in a market.

The butcher turned to Nasir and said, "It is your turn."

Reluctantly, Nasir was forced to take part in the savage butchery when they handed him a chainsaw and he was told to kill Jo-Jo. The machine roared in his hands. He glared at Jo-Jo and for a split second saw Shoe-Shine. Jo-Jo was shivering with pure panic. He wasn't used to hacking a man apart with knives and chainsaws. He wasn't used to this kind of murder. In his eyes it was inhumane. In the hood, you used a gun and put a few bullets into your victim and it was over with. You literally didn't have blood on your hands.

He thought the Colombians were savages.

Nasir stepped closer to Jo-Jo, who was still on his knees and bonded with thick rope that cut into his wrists. He squirmed and peed on himself. His eyes were red with fear and tears.

"Nasir, please, don't do this! Don't do this to me, man! Please!" Jo-Jo screamed hysterically. "No! No! I don't wanna die!"

"He needs to die, Nasir," said the butcher.

Nasir frowned. Even though he was betrayed by Jo-Jo, this type of killing wasn't his forte. But he didn't have a choice. Nasir neared the chainsaw to the naked Jo-Jo and revved the engine. It was a fearsome sound that wailed in his victim's ears, causing his eyes to widen with terror. Jo-Jo continued to beg for his life, but his pleas fell on deaf ears. The chainsaw shredded into his neck with his blood splattering out like a gusher, causing him to shudder and scream violently from the pain.

Steadily, the teeth from the saw sliced through flesh and bone, eventually beheading Jo-Jo. When he was done, Nasir couldn't look at the body. He was covered in the man's blood and he felt sick to his stomach.

"Buen trabajo," the butcher uttered. "It's in your blood, Nasir."

Does he think this is funny? Nasir thought. He stood frozen with disbelief at what he had done. He dropped the chainsaw and stepped outside to get a breath of fresh air.

For the next two hours, Nasir contributed in cutting up the bodies of each victim for disposal. They were dropped in barrels of acid and dissolved by the chemical. The Colombians definitely did things differently from him and his own Brooklyn goons.

Nasir was starting to grow weary of so many things.

While he was looking lost in space, the men around him were laughing and joking like it was all a game. They were used to this kind of inhumane type of butchery. Nasir just wanted to go back home and take his mind away from the things he saw.

The ride back to New York was a quiet and a challenging one for Nasir. It had been a very long night. The butchery of five men, including Jo-Jo, was something he would never forget. He arrived in Brooklyn before dawn and had nothing else to say to anyone. The acting boss of the men handed Nasir a bundle of money—ten stacks for his services. Nasir took the cash, but he was feeling ambivalent about so many things. When the Tahoe drove away, Nasir stood next to his car for a moment and smoked a cigarette. In his mind, he thought about his own fate with the cartel. Would his fate be the same way once they were done with him?

Nasir took a few strong pulls and got into his Benz. He called home.

"What's up, baby?"

"It's late. Where are you?" Fancy asked.

"I'm in the streets."

"You comin' home?"

"I want to, but I'm dead tired. I'm so fuckin' exhausted. I think I'ma stay at my mom's crib and head home in the a.m."

"You sure?"

"I want to come home, but things gotta change, Fancy." Nasir was ready to start an argument. He felt unloved, used, confused, and lost.

"Oh fuckin' boy, not again." Fancy sucked her teeth. "I'll see you in the morning."

She hung up.

Nasir was going to call right back and apologize but decided to do it in person. Instead of going into his mother's apartment, he decided to commit to the long drive to the estate in Long Island. As he drove, he thought about the money, the murders, the cars, his prestige and clout, and it wasn't what he'd felt it would be. Things were changing, and it wasn't for the better.

It was nearing dawn when Nasir pulled into the driveway. His eyes were bloodshot red from driving the hour from Brooklyn to Long Island, and being part of a bloody massacre.

He entered the unhappy home and headed to their bedroom. From the end of the hallway he heard moaning coming from the master bedroom. Nasir pulled out his pistol and slowly headed toward that direction. The closer he came to the room, the louder the moaning and panting became. He was very familiar with the tone. It sounded like his bitch was cheating on him. He was ready to kill the unlucky bastard that was sticking dick into his lady. It would be the last piece of pussy the bastard ever would have on earth. Nasir puckered his brow and gripped the gun tightly. When he got to the bedroom, he noticed the door was ajar. Nasir looked inside and what he saw truly stunned him.

He witnessed his girlfriend, Fancy, engaged in a threesome with Pippa and another woman. It was a lesbian orgy. Each girl moaned heatedly and they were so absorbed in each other that they didn't notice Nasir staring from the doorway. Upset, Nasir outstretched his arm with the gun at the end of it and aimed. He wanted to interrupt their love affair with shots fired. He was seething with rage and ready to take action.

At one time, he actually loved Fancy. But at that moment, he despised her and everything that she had turned into. Nasir decided not to say a word and lowered his gun. They didn't see him at all, because they were so engrossed in bumping and rubbing pussies together. Nasir backed out of the room and left the house. The three whores could have he each other, he thought, and they would never realize how close they came to death.

Nasir climbed back into his Benz and left. He made the decision to go back to where his true home was—Brooklyn. He was done with Fancy.

CHAPTER 17

Belen sat on her cot in her cramped six-by-eight-foot prison cell with steel walls and a solid door that locked from the outside. There was one rectangular window that allowed sunlight in. Furnishing and fixtures inside the cell were constructed so that they couldn't easily be broken and were anchored to the walls and floor. And there was a stainless-steel sink and commode.

She didn't have a cellmate, which was the one blessing for now. With so much going on in the outside world, Belen couldn't stop worrying about her daughter. She couldn't shake or figure out how word had gotten out about who Fancy's biological father really was. Fancy assured her that she hadn't told a soul. Then who did, and why? It baffled her. Daily she tried to put two and two together, and then it suddenly dawned on her who told and the reason why.

Belen needed to see and speak to Fancy immediately. It was a matter of life and death.

Once again, Fancy found herself seated across from Belen in the visiting room. Every time she kept saying it was going to be her last visit, it wasn't. She just couldn't keep away from her mother, no matter how much Belen would upset her. No matter what, she was still her mother and she knew the streets, the cartels, and the underworld. Fancy had to respect her mother, because she flourished in that life for a very long time and had survived. She couldn't say the same thing about Alexandro and so many others who were cut down by violence.

"I'm glad you came to see me, Fancy. You look really nice," Belen said politely, complimenting Fancy on the white Gucci dress and belt she wore.

Fancy was somewhat taken aback by her mother's pleasant demeanor all of a sudden. She was used to Belen calling her dumb bitches and scowling. What had changed her? Fancy asked herself.

"Thank you," Fancy replied, graciously.

No matter what, Fancy knew she still needed Belen in her life. In some strange way, even from behind the prison walls, Belen became her advisor and confidant. Besides Pippa, her mother was the next woman in her life she could talk to, even when things got heated between them. Belen always kept it real, and told her the truth—post FBI raid.

"You need to know something, Fancy. I've been trying to be forthright with you, and it won't end with what I have to tell you," said Belen.

"Okay . . . what is it?" Fancy asked wryly.

Belen gave her daughter a steely look and said, "I believe that somehow Jesus has to be the one who put the word out about you being his biological daughter."

"And this is a problem, how? I mean, this is good news for me, Mommy. It means that he's finally accepting me being his daughter. I don't understand why you seem scared. I'm tired of hiding everything. I'm not you. I don't want to hide anything from anyone, like you did to me all those years."

"You don't understand, Fancy. This man doesn't care about you at all. You need to wake up and see how dangerous and sinister Jesus can be."

"How dangerous?" It was a rhetorical question coming from Fancy. She didn't believe anything her mother was telling her.

"He's using you, Fancy. He needs you to lure the killers of his other beloved children," Belen informed her bluntly.

"What the fuck are you talking about? You trying to say that I'm nothing to him but bait?" Fancy barked. She became enraged at the thought.

"Yes," Belen replied frankly.

"I don't believe you!"

If it wasn't one thing, then it was another with Belen. Fancy couldn't believe what she was hearing. Her father? The man she had warmed up to, and who had probably warmed up to her—and who also had an open door policy to visit him whenever she needed to talk about anything. Jesus even hugged her once. Though it was brief, it was still a hug from him.

Fancy truly felt that her father would never use her life to catch the ones responsible for his other daughters' murders. She was his daughter, too. So what would make them more precious than Fancy?

"Stop being so damn blind, Fancy," Belen added. "You can be so fuckin' stupid!"

"Why are you doing this to me?" Fancy asked.

Bait? Fancy didn't see it. But Belen was determined to make her believe it. She stared at Fancy and carefully explained the details to her.

"I was nothing but a fling to Jesus, an attractive black woman that he wanted to experiment sexually with. I was attracted to him. He was a very handsome man. He wouldn't admit it, but he fell in love with me. But we both were smart enough to know that it would never work. And unfortunately, I found out that I was pregnant with you. He only kept me alive when I made a vow to him that I would keep the pregnancy a secret and would never reveal who my baby's true father was.

"See, you're a half-breed, Fancy; not pure Colombian blood like his other two daughters. You will never be one of them. I don't care what you think. Jesus' two daughters were conceived by his first wife, who had six

163

miscarriages—they were all boys—before the first girl lived. Her name was Marisol. And then the second full-term pregnancy was Maribel. Both of his children were a hundred percent Colombian, and you're not. You are a bastard child with black blood running through your veins, and therefore, Jesus will never completely accept you as his. You need to accept the fucking truth, Fancy. It's a facade with him. And when he's finished with you, he will discard you like you're nothing but trash."

"You're a fuckin' liar!" Fancy screamed out. "What year is this? No one cares about full or half-breed blood. Please!"

The truth was harsh and Fancy couldn't accept it. She was overwhelmed with rage, and within the blink of an eye, she lunged across the table.

Belen fell back and out of the chair. She recovered quickly and began throwing blows to Fancy's head and face. Fancy tried to defend herself from the onslaught of blows. The guards quickly stormed over and pulled Belen off of Fancy.

"I hate you! I fuckin' hate you! You're a liar!" Fancy shouted, still defiant.

"How dare you put your fuckin' hands on me?" Belen countered. "You could never handle the truth—that's why we always kept it from you. You're a dead woman, Fancy, if you believe that man truly loves you. He doesn't! He's ruthless!"

"I'm not you, Mommy! I'm his daughter, and I know he cares for me!"

"Don't be a silly bitch, Fancy. Be careful."

Everyone, including the guards, was taken aback by the fight between mother and daughter, especially being aware of Belen's reputation. The guards pulled Fancy away from the room and had to detain her for disorderly conduct and violence in a federal building. She was processed and held overnight for the assault. But while she sat in the small holding cell, seething, she vowed to never go see her mother again—enough was enough. From this day on, Belen was dead to her.

CHAPTER 18

Being back in Miami made Esmeralda want to kick off her shoes, sip on a large cocktail and make love to her beautiful girlfriend, Sexy. The sun-drenched city was more beautiful than ever. New York was a rude and boisterous city, and she wanted to stay away from it for a moment and enjoy the Sunshine State like she always did. But she was on a mission, and she would make the Big Apple her second home if she had to in order to stay close to her target.

Esmeralda was very proud of herself. She had infiltrated Fancy's circle and was becoming a close friend to her. It didn't take too long for the two to start up a love affair—what woman or man could resist Esmeralda's beauty? They always had an itch to try it out with her sexually—she was a sex kitten. And Fancy became another notch on her belt when it came to turning a bitch out. The young woman was tasty and so sweet in the bed, that Esmeralda almost hated that she had to kill her. But she vowed to erase Pablo and anyone protecting him.

She had been traveling from New York to Miami repeatedly and handling her business for several weeks now. She always had to make sure that her home was well taken care of, and it was. But in between her traveling, she kept close to Fancy and pushed to meet with her connect. It was a subtle approach; she knew not to push too hard. She didn't want

Fancy becoming suspicious of her true motive. So during their time together in New York, having girl talk in some of Manhattan's most affluent locations, they would chit-chat and Esmeralda would shrewdly ask questions about her family. She wanted Fancy to open up more, and it was working, but it was taking time—maybe too much time.

Revenge was a bitch best served cold, and it was going to feel like ice water had been dumped on Fancy once Esmeralda was done with her. While in New York, she had gotten Fancy to confide about her past life. They were in Fancy's Long Island home and seated by the pool once again. She wanted to get into Fancy's head and get as much information out of her as possible. She was the key to getting at Jesus and then Pablo. Fancy was the last living piece to his heritage, but that was about to change.

Fancy had been going through a lot. Nasir had disappeared from her life without any reasonable explanation, and it worried her. Her calls were unanswered and it seemed like he had completely vanished from her life. She went by her aunt Brenda's house on several occasions looking for him but he was never there. But she soon heard through the grapevine that Nasir was back with his old Harlem bitch. Hearing this infuriated Fancy.

And then the fight with her mother was still upsetting. Fancy felt alone—like she had no one. Her family was abandoning her. Now with Nasir fucking around with his tramp bitch uptown and Belen no longer a mother to her, she was truly on her own. And the predicament that Fancy was in gave "Pippa" the chance to swoop in and take advantage of it.

The two talked straightforwardly about their past. Esmeralda made sure to share stories about her family and her love life, but they were fabricated. It was the doorway of trust for Fancy. The next thing she knew, Fancy started confiding to Pippa about her mother and Nasir. Everything about Belen troubled Fancy and she let it slip out about her mother being in the MDC prison and her father, Alexandro, being murdered in the MCC prison while he was awaiting trial. Pippa thought Fancy would talk about her real father, Jesus, but she never did.

"Why was your father murdered?" she had asked Fancy.

"I don't know. I do know he was set up. He was a really good man and he loved me a lot," she had confided.

"A father's love is always the best."

"It is."

The two talked until the sun started to fade from the sky. She wanted to know more about Fancy's connect. While they were having drinks, she went on to say, "This connect of yours, how long have you been with him?"

Fancy looked reluctant to answer the question. "Why do you want to know? What difference does it make?"

"I was just asking, Fancy. You know me, I'm very cautious with the people I deal with."

"So am I," Fancy returned.

Fancy raised her brow, becoming somewhat suspicious of Pippa's questions. It wasn't the first time that Pippa brought up her connect. And then there were the sudden questions about her family. She thought that her only ally was Pippa, but Fancy was hardly a fool. She began to realize that Pippa was asking too many questions about her pedigree, about her family, and trying to be shrewd with her approach. But yet, Fancy didn't truly know anything about Pippa—she wondered if the stories her newfound friend was telling her could be fake. She had vetted Pippa, but something was wrong.

Fancy came up with the absurd idea that Pippa was planted into her life by her father, Jesus, to spy on her. But if so, then why?

Soon, it would become a game of cat and mouse between them. Pippa wasn't as subtle as she thought she was. Fancy was a different ballgame to be played, and she'd learned from the best—her parents.

Esmeralda lingered around her lavish Miami condo with a tequila cocktail in her hand. In Miami, she was ready to take care of her business. It was a beautiful afternoon, but there was so much work that had to be done that she didn't have time to enjoy the beaches or nightclubs.

She was aware of the sudden change in Fancy's attitude toward her. Somehow, Fancy had become suspicious of her. She didn't like it. She had slipped up somewhere, maybe asking too many questions about her connect or family. Maybe Fancy had a change of heart about their friendship. But Fancy was smarter than Esmeralda had expected, and being in Miami, she had to come up with a different approach. She had come too close to let the big fish slip out of her hand.

Esmeralda walked out onto the immense terrace where the striking view of the Miami skyline put her mind someplace wonderful for the moment. She took a few sips from her cocktail, untied her robe, and let it fall from her shoulders to around her feet and revealed her bikini-clad body. She gazed out at the picturesque view of the sun setting over the city and exhaled.

She couldn't stop thinking about Fancy..Esmeralda felt the young girl gradually distancing herself from their newfound friendship. Before she left New York, she'd tried to link up with Fancy, but Fancy would steadily come up with an excuse why she couldn't. It was upsetting Esmeralda and she had to change up the strategy. She tried it the nice way, and now it was time to play it her way—hard.

While Esmeralda relaxed on the terrace, the front door to her lavish high-rise opened and Sexy came walking in. She was excited to see her lover again. This time, Esmeralda had been gone for almost a month, and it was taking a toll on their relationship. Seeing Esmeralda out on the terrace in her two-piece bikini turned Sexy on. As she walked toward her lover, she peeled away the white minidress she wore and went to greet Esmeralda in her panties.

"Hey baby, I missed you so much." Sexy greeted Esmeralda with a longing kiss.

"I missed you too," Esmeralda replied.

The two quickly locked lips once they were near each other, and then they started to grope each other like young teens in the back of a car. Esmeralda ran her hands across Sexy's shapely hips. Her touch was gentle, but her eyes were eager to taste and feel every inch of Sexy's body. Both of their lips were like sweet strawberries and their bodies were soft like clouds. The ladies couldn't wait to devour each other.

The gentle kisses against Sexy's brown skin, along with the firm touching, was exhilarating. Immediately, Esmeralda's pussy began to throb and pulsate. The two walked back into the living room and Esmeralda took to the floor and lay on her back. Sexy kissed her way toward Esmeralda's precious honey spot, tasting her lover slowly and pressing her full lips to all of Esmeralda's erotic places.

"Ooooh, baby, that feels so good," Esmeralda cooed.

Sexy licked everywhere, methodically. She sucked on Esmeralda's nipples and licked her gently.

Sexy kissed in between her thighs and was ready to dive into her pussy. Sexy took her fingers and gently spread Esmeralda's pink lips and started to finger her pussy tenderly. Esmeralda squirmed with her legs spread eagle style, grinding her pussy into Sexy's face. She felt Sexy's tongue wiggle inside of her with the simultaneous thrusting of her fingers into her pussy. It was an overwhelming feeling for them both.

"Ooooh shit, baby . . . don't stop, just like that. It feels so good, baby," Esmeralda cooed.

Sexy went from sucking Esmeralda's pussy to sucking on her tits and nipples with their bodies entwined and fervent kisses lasting for several minutes. The two took turns doing each other zealously with their moans echoing out and their pussies dripping with pleasure—each girl licking, kissing, rubbing, and sucking each other to several powerful orgasms.

Shortly after, both of them embraced each other, looking pleased and spent. Sexy stared at Esmeralda and said, "Welcome home, baby. I definitely missed you."

Esmeralda smiled and replied, "I see, it showed."

The two shared a laugh. But Esmeralda let it be known that she was leaving again in a few days to take action against Fancy.

"When?" Sexy asked.

"Sometime next week, and this time, I'm doing things the hard way. I'm sick of playing nice with this young bitch. She ain't on my level and will never be. And it's time to cut her down," Esmeralda declared.

"I'm coming with you," Sexy said.

"You don't need to."

"Yes, I do. If anything ever happened to you, I'd go crazy and a lot of people would die," Sexy said with certainty.

Esmeralda didn't argue with her. She might come in handy in a time of need.

CHAPTER 19

F ancy had so many things to worry about on her way to meet with Jesus
for the umpteenth time in several months. But she couldn't dwell on
everything, especially the theory her mother had about her being bait for
Jesus to bring out the killers of his two daughters. Also, thinking about
Nasir being with another woman hurt her more. Still, she had an empire
to run and product to move.

Fancy exited her Long Island home alone. It was dusk out and a
warm night. She was armed with a .380 concealed on her person. Clad
in a short-sleeved minidress and her stylish heels, she climbed into her
BMW, started the ignition, and drove out the large driveway. It was a long
drive into Manhattan, but she was eager to meet with Jesus once again.
She always went alone.

She thought about revealing to him that she knew the truth, and
feeling him out. She had the urge to ask Jesus what the real deal with her
and him was—did he care for her at all? She would hate to know that her
mother was right about everything.

She made a right onto the side street and headed toward the highway
while listening to Shade 45 on SiriusXM. But as Fancy drove, a pair of
headlights behind her caught her immediate attention. Was someone
following her, or was she becoming paranoid? She was alone and affiliated

with a high-profile figure in the underworld. He had enemies. She had haters. To make sure she wasn't being followed, she made another right onto a narrow road and bypassed merging onto the Long Island Expressway. When she made a third right, the car following behind her did the same. She learned how to pick up a tail from Nasir. He taught her some techniques and they were coming in handy at the moment.

The headlights were two cars behind her, trying to be inconspicuous, but it didn't work. Fancy was sure she was being followed. She was on a private road and needed to get to a public venue quickly. It was obvious that someone was after her. Feeling frantic, the first person she called was Nasir.

"Baby, pick up . . . please pick up." Fancy held the cell phone to her ear, and her eyes diverted back and forth from the road to the car following her. Unfortunately, the call went straight to voicemail. "Fuck!"

Fancy sped up a little. She removed the .380, took off the safety, and kept it close. She became more alert. She made another turn and headed in the direction of the mall. A few miles away, her cell phone rang. When she saw Nasir's name on the caller I.D, some relief came over her. She quickly answered, but shockingly it wasn't Nasir but his girlfriend returning the phone call.

"Bitch, why the fuck you calling my man for?" a female voice cursed at her.

Fancy didn't have time for this shit. "Where's Nas?" she exclaimed.

"He don't have time for you, and I would fuckin' appreciate if you didn't call his phone anymore!"

"Bitch, you know who you're talking to?" Fancy shouted.

"I know, and I ain't scared of you, bitch! I'm his woman now, and I know how to take care of my man—unlike you!" she barked.

What the fuck was Nasir telling this bitch? But she didn't have time for a shouting match with the next bitch; her life was in danger and she had to think fast. The call went dead. It was obvious the woman hung up. Fancy didn't need to call back. She had to figure out how to survive tonight.

Fancy said to herself, fuck it, and she accelerated at a high speed and went speeding through the streets. If push came to shove, she would get pulled over by police, and despite her hatred for cops, it would be a temporary blessing. She went flying through a red light, nearly causing a three-car accident, and then made a right hairpin turn onto the next street. Her adrenaline was up and running. She gripped the .380 and looked in her rearview mirror. She saw nothing. She had eluded the car following her, or so she thought. She still decided to drive to the mall and get her mind right. For now, it was safer for her to be in a public area—lots of people and police. No one would be crazy enough to try her there.

Fancy pulled into the parking lot of Green Acres Mall, thirty-five miles from her home. It was getting late; the mall was going to close in an hour. She parked her car near the entrance and got out. The area was still bustling with people coming and going. The parking lot was inundated with cars.

Fancy concealed her .380, and before she stepped forward to go anywhere, she made a few phone calls to some of her henchmen and let them know where to meet her. They would be there in a half-hour. Fancy took a deep breath and walked toward the mall entrance. She tried to look calm and collected. She strode toward the mall giving off strength and confidence. Whoever was after her, chances were they wouldn't find her here.

But before Fancy could get inside, she heard her name being called.

"Fancy! Fancy!" a woman shouted.

Fancy was familiar with the voice. She turned around to see Pippa approaching her in a silver Audi S8. Fancy was surprised to see Pippa back in town, and of all places, at Green Acres Mall in Long Island. Pippa wasn't alone. There was another female in the car with her. She didn't seem too friendly and frowned at Fancy like she was the Antichrist or something. Fancy gazed at the two.

"Pippa, I'm surprised to see you here," Fancy said evenly.

"I know, I was just in the area and happened to see you walking by. Funny thing, huh? It's a small world after all."

"Yeah, funny thing, and it is, a very small world."

"Why you here so late?" Pippa asked.

"I'm just out here taking care of some business."

"Oh, what business is that?" Pippa asked.

"Just business," Fancy replied, being short with her. "Shopping."

"You alone?"

"Not really. You know I'm always with my peoples," Fancy replied.

"Yeah, I know. I just don't see them around."

"They are," Fancy assured them, bluffing to the highest degree.

"But Fancy, why don't you come take a ride with us and let's get the party started?" Pippa suggested.

"What?"

"I love New York so much that I came right back. Let's go get something to eat and have drinks."

"Tonight?" Fancy questioned with her raised brow. It didn't seem right to her at all. Fancy kept her hand near her pistol just in case something jumped off. Her heart was beating fast and she was itching to make a run for it. It felt like something bad was about to happen and Pippa was going to be the cause of it.

"Why not tonight? It's not like it needs to be a special occasion to hang out with girlfriends."

"Who's ya homegirl?" Fancy asked.

"Michelle, Fancy . . . Fancy, Michelle," Pippa introduced them halfheartedly.

It was obvious that Michelle and Fancy didn't care for each other. Michelle looked cynical. She stared at Fancy like she was ready to whip her ass.

"I'm gonna take a rain check, Pippa. I'm kind of busy tonight. But we can link up some other time. You got my number."

"Yeah, I do."

"So call me," Fancy replied dryly.

Pippa smirked. She was ready to jump out the car and kidnap Fancy with Sexy's help. She couldn't wait any longer for the moment. Fancy had to die tonight, but not before they tortured her to reveal any information she knew about Jesus or Pablo. They believed she knew something to lead them in the right direction, and no matter how they did it, she was going to talk.

Pippa shook her head; her demeanor was creepy and somewhat inhospitable. Fancy caught bad vibes from both ladies in the car. Pippa's eyes seemed shifty. Fancy knew her suspicion of being followed was correct. It had to be Pippa that was following her. She knew her home address, and why didn't Pippa let her know that she was back in town? Something wasn't right, and Fancy felt the threat. The moment between them was awkward, and both females realized they'd blown their cover.

Fancy pivoted and headed back in the direction of her parked car.

"I thought you was going to the mall, Fancy," Pippa said.

"I forgot something in the car." Fancy hurried toward her Benz, moving briskly between all the parked cars and crossing the lane with the keys already in her hand and deactivating the alarm system. She could feel Pippa's eyes on her with hatred. They were about to pull off something bold, and Fancy wasn't going to be a victim tonight.

Pippa put the Audi in reverse, knowing Fancy wasn't coming back to the mall, and she tried to maneuver the car to prevent Fancy's escape. The engine of the Audio S8 roared like thunder. Fancy jumped into her AMG

Benz and hit the ignition; she thrust the gear into drive and sped out of the parking lot, nearly hitting an oncoming car. It was a tight escape, but Fancy was determined to get away.

She made a sharp left and from the rearview mirror saw Pippa trying to catch up to her. Fancy gunned it, and made the mistake of sideswiping an oncoming car trying to leave the parking lot in a hurry. It was a hit-and-run, but Fancy didn't have time to stop and apologize to the driver. She continued driving, becoming Jeff Gordon behind the wheel. She made it to the main street and dipped in and out of traffic like a stunt driver on a movie set.

Looking into her rearview mirror once more, she didn't see the Audi S8 pursuing her, so she assumed she lost Pippa and her friend. It seemed that her Benz AMG was just too fast for the Audi S8. Fancy was able to breathe a little, but she was still in danger. Fancy raced toward Brooklyn. Her meeting with Jesus had to be put on hold for the moment. The last thing she wanted to do was bring any danger his way. She decided to go see her Aunt Brenda. She couldn't get in contact with Nasir, so she was the next best thing.

Fancy made it into Brooklyn in no time. She came to a stop in front of her aunt's building and hopped out. It had been a minute since she'd come to see her. The locals and thugs were all out on a balmy summer night. A few men were gambling on the corner and getting high from haze. When they noticed the gleaming AMG parking on their block, all activity stopped and the occupant of the luxury car became the primary focus. Looking like a diamond in a rough, Fancy strutted toward the front entrance with hordes of eyes watching her.

"Hey, Fancy," a neighbor called out.

Fancy remained nonchalant and nodded. She didn't have time to socialize or reminisce with anyone. She used to be a familiar face not too long ago, but since she came up, she wanted to make Brooklyn a memory.

The beauty queen seemed fearless in the rowdy neighborhood. Everyone knew who she was—either she was known as Nasir's cousin, which she really wasn't, or she was Nasir's main bitch, and they dared not to disrespect her at all. Fancy entered the building with a straight face. The men could look, but they couldn't touch.

Fancy moved through the lobby and made her way up the stairs. She seemed immune to the foul smell and dilapidated conditions of the tenement building. This had been her home for many months, and residing in such horrid conditions had only strengthened her.

Fancy walked toward Brenda's apartment. Everything seemed quiet inside. She knocked loudly. It didn't take long for Brenda to shout out, "Who is it?" She sounded ghetto fabulous.

"Aunt Brenda, it's me, Fancy."

There was a quick hesitation and then Fancy heard the locks being turned from the inside. The door opened up and Brenda stood in front of her niece in a blue housecoat and slippers. Her hair was in rollers. It seemed like she was ready to go out tonight and Fancy had caught her at a bad time.

"Brenda, we need to talk. Can I come in?" Fancy quickly said.

"You know you're always welcome here, Fancy," Brenda replied.

Brenda felt she didn't have a choice. The look she saw in Fancy's eyes told her that something had spooked her. Brenda stepped to the side and allowed Fancy to walk into her lavishly decorated apartment, credit to the drug game.

Closing the door behind her, Fancy didn't take a seat. She looked at her aunt with apprehension and said, "I got trouble, Aunt Brenda."

"What kind of trouble?"

"This bitch named Pippa tried to come at me earlier. She followed me from my home to the mall."

"Who is she?" Brenda asked.

"I befriended her a few months back, and we did business together. But now something's up with her and I think she's a front. And I don't know if someone placed her into my life to spy on me or if she's from a rival crew trying to set me up," Fancy said, exasperated. "I tried to call your son, but he's not accepting or returning any of my phone calls."

"Fancy, this is out of my hands. Why did you come here? You need to go and speak to your mother about this."

"I can't. We're not speaking right now."

"Why not?" asked Brenda.

"Cuz, she can be a fuckin' bitch! Just as you've always said."

"So, what do you expect me to do?" Brenda asked.

"I need your help, Aunt Brenda," Fancy exclaimed.

"And how I'm supposed to help you? You're the queen-pin out there with the goons and a cartel backing you. You and Nasir knew what you were getting into. I mean, I would never turn my back on either one of you, but I don't have an army, guns, or fuck-you-money stashed away. I'm a mother of five, Fancy, and I have to keep the little ones safe. What you need is Belen."

"But you are turning your back on me! After everything I did for you, you owe me, Aunt Brenda. And besides, I can't reach your son. He's not picking up his phone for me."

"I helped you when you first came to my door wit' nuthin'. I took you in, and I did my part for you, Fancy. What more can I do for you? You really need to go and speak to your mother. I don't care how upset you are wit' her, my sister might know best."

Fancy caught an attitude. Going to see her mother again was not an option. She had to find another alternative. "I need to know where Nasir is," Fancy demanded. "Where is he?"

"He's in Harlem, and you truly do need to go see him. That's the best idea you came up wit' yet," Brenda replied.

Brenda also encouraged Fancy to try and get Nasir back from his current girlfriend in Harlem. Brenda talked to her son on a regular and she explained to Fancy how sick he was without her. It was hard to believe that Nasir could show any emotion, because he could be so cold and distant. But Brenda confirmed he did truly miss her.

Fancy spent several hours at her aunt's place. She planned on reconnecting with Nasir as soon as possible. It had been several weeks since he'd walked out of her life, and she needed him more than ever.

CHAPTER 20

Fancy pulled up to the towering project buildings—the Harlem River Housing on 151st Street and Harlem River Drive. She stepped out of her car and gazed up at the building that Nasir was temporarily residing in. She couldn't believe her man had the audacity to leave her and their Long Island estate to slum it with a bum bitch in a Harlem project. He was connected to a cartel, and it was embarrassing to her organization.

Fancy walked through the projects, fearless, though she was a stranger to the notorious hood. She knew nothing about Harlem. Entering the building, Fancy took the elevator up to the fifth floor and looked for the apartment number that Brenda had given to her. She didn't know what to expect when she knocked on the door. She came prepared for anything with her .380. She was bold enough to knock on the door and confront this bitch.

The apartment door opened up and Fancy stood face to face with some redbone, leggy bitch with long blonde hair. She looked fiercely at Fancy and exclaimed, "Bitch, what you want?"

"I'm here to see Nasir. Where is he?" Fancy refuted.

"He ain't tryin' to see you, bitch!"

Fancy frowned heavily. She was ready to barge into the apartment to see Nasir and drag him out if she had to. She needed to talk to him.

But his bitch looked feisty and ignorant. Fancy didn't have time to argue and fuss with someone she deemed beneath her. She needed to see Nasir, and she wasn't leaving until they talked. Without warning, Fancy balled her fists, lunged forward and punched the blonde woman in the head, causing her to stumble. Fancy was all over her like white on rice, yanking her weave out and causing havoc in the hallway.

"You fuckin' bitch!" the blonde woman screamed out.

The two went to blows, yelling and screaming in the hallway and causing neighbors to emerge from their apartments to see what the fuss was about. Seeing two young girls fighting in the narrow hallway was a shock to them. Fancy proved to be a better fighter than she thought. She poured her rage and anger out like a stream and had the other woman against the floor with a bloody lip and busted nose. She repeatedly beat her down with her fists and was ready to cripple her if necessary.

A shirtless Nasir rushed toward the fight and roughly pulled both ladies apart. He shouted, "What the fuck are y'all doin'?"

It took help from another male neighbor to restrain Fancy. She was a pit bull in a skirt and was ready to tear the girl apart.

Nasir glared at Fancy and exclaimed, "What the fuck are you doin' here, Fancy?"

"We need to talk," she cried out.

"We have nuthin' to talk about," Nasir retorted.

"Fuck that bitch! I'ma kill that fuckin' bitch!" the woman shouted.

Nasir turned and looked angrily at her and scolded, "Chill the fuck out! Believe me, this the one bitch you don't wanna fuck wit'."

The woman scowled heavily and kept quiet. But her look toward Fancy was murderous. Fancy returned the same murderous look, and she didn't shout out idle threats—it was too simple to have this woman's life snatched away. But she didn't have time to involve herself with ghetto-ass bitches. Nasir was her main focus.

"Nasir, please, I really need to talk to you. It's very important," Fancy said, almost pleading to him.

Nasir looked reluctant to leave with her. He looked at Fancy and then looked at Meeka. Meeka had her hands on her hips and grimaced, almost daring Nasir to leave with his ex-bitch.

"Nasir, I know you ain't really thinkin' 'bout leaving wit' this stank bitch," Meeka hollered.

He looked at Fancy and said, "Give me a minute, and let me go put on a shirt."

He went into the apartment leaving Meeka dumbfounded. Fancy smirked. Meeka looked like she was ready to lunge at Fancy. But Fancy was ready to go for a round two. The ladies only glared at each other with a tall male neighbor standing between them, trying to keep the peace in his building.

Nasir came out the apartment fully dressed.

"Nasir, I know you ain't tryin' to just leave like that," Meeka shouted. "You's a foul muthafucka then! Fuck you! After I give you some of this good pussy, you just gonna bounce after ya ex disrespects me and come knockin' on my fuckin' door? Fuck you, nigga! Fuck you!"

Nasir didn't pay Meeka any attention. He left with Fancy so they could have a heart-to-heart talk. They took the elevator down to the lobby and walked toward Fancy's Benz. She was driving. They sped away and headed toward the highway. The duration of the ride was quiet, somewhat awkward. Both had a lot to think about. They went and parked near the George Washington Bridge. Fancy and Nasir gazed at the Hudson River and the New Jersey shore across the river for a moment. It was a beautiful night.

Fancy turned and fixed her attention on Nasir. He pulled out a cigarette, lit it, and inhaled the nicotine. He was so handsome—and such a thug, very street-smart and crazy. It bothered her that he had fucked that bitch in the project, but she couldn't argue about it. They both made mistakes.

"Why did you leave, Nasir?" Fancy bluntly asked.

"Honestly, because you was fuckin' wit' my manhood and you let this shit wit' the cartels go to your head. And then, that bitch Pippa—I don't trust her, and never will. I saw you wit' her—the threesome y'all were having in the bedroom. I coulda took each and every last one of y'all out, but I didn't. But ya slippin', Fancy, and gettin' caught up. You think I need that shit in my life? You think I can afford to risk everything for your carelessness? Do you?" he demanded heatedly.

Fancy was shocked and most shocked that he knew about her and Pippa. "I'm sorry."

"It ain't about being fuckin' sorry. It's about being careful, before you really become sorry. I've been in the streets much longer than you, and just because Jesus made you into some goddess in this game, you still don't know shit. Yeah, ya smart wit' ya businesses and networking, I'll give you that . . . but when it comes to this street shit, ya naive and reckless wit' it. This is my world, and I grew up in it. You was fuckin' born wit' a silver spoon in ya mouth, and you think you better than me."

"My life was threatened," Fancy let him know. It was the only thing she could say to him at the moment.

Hearing this news made Nasir change his tone toward her a little. He frowned. "By who?" he questioned with alarm.

"Pippa."

Nasir became infuriated. "I told you not to trust that fuckin' bitch! I told ya ass, didn't I? What happened?"

"She came at me in the mall parking lot and she had some other bitch with her. She was either going to shoot me there or try and kidnap me. I barely got away and went to see your mother. She gave me your location. I needed to come see you."

"You should have never brought her into the loop in the first place. You sure you wasn't followed?"

"No, I wasn't. I stayed over Aunt Brenda's the entire night."

"So you put my moms in danger? And Al-Saadiq, Lisa and the twins? What the fuck is wrong wit' you?"

"I was careful, I swear. And I needed to find you."

Nasir exhaled. "You need to tell me everything that happened."

Fancy was ready to break down in front of him. She was rapidly overcome with emotions. Just the thought of allowing such a high risk into her home and Pippa almost having the upper hand on her was too scary to think of. She vetted the woman, but somehow, her true identity or motive slipped through the cracks and Fancy hadn't been as careful as she'd thought she was.

"I fucked up, okay? I admit that. I was on my way to meet with Jesus. She followed me from the house, I tried to elude her, but I didn't. And the only reason I fucked her that night, was because I was drunk and not myself. I told her that I wasn't gay and that I was strictly dickly, but that bitch doesn't take rejection too well," Fancy said.

"First, ya not goin' back to that house anymore. We changing locations, we get more goons out and then we find out who this bitch really is. You talked to Jesus?"

"No."

"You need to. Maybe he may know sumthin' about this bitch and why the sudden appearance in your life. And you need to visit your mother."

"She's dead to me."

"Oh, grow up," Nasir declared. "You need to go see her, Fancy, and let her know what's goin' on. This shit is real right now, and the more info we can get about anything, the better."

Fancy was adamant about not visiting her mother. She was done with Belen. But Brenda and Nasir were telling her the same thing.

"Don't be stubborn about this shit, Fancy. All this shit don't make sense. We gotta find out who this bitch really is and then we go after her."

Fancy stared at Nasir. He was her man. He was cool and collected. And the way he was taking charge over the situation made Fancy realize that her true love was with him. She had been so blinded by power and Pippa, that she almost ruined a good thing with him, if not already. The way Nasir acted showed that he truly cared and loved her.

"I love you so much, Nasir. I'm so sorry about everything. I'm sorry for the way I've treated you. I need you, baby. I do." Fancy felt the tears about to pour from her eyes.

Nasir looked at her. He then leaned toward her, his steely look softening to some extent. He took her hand in his, and his touch comforted Fancy. She would always be his queen. He couldn't stay away forever. But now that she'd come to her senses, Nasir was ready to commit to the woman he fell in love with the day she arrived at his mother's apartment looking lost and scared.

He took a deep breath and replied, "I love you, too, baby. And we're in this together, fifty-fifty, you and me. And remember this, I'm ya fuckin' man, not ya damn servant. You treat me wit' fuckin' respect out here like the streets do, cuz I'm the one that's gonna always have ya back. You understand me?"

Fancy nodded.

A few tears trickled from her eyes. Nasir wiped them away with the back of his hand. They stared at each other and were ready to recommit into something stronger than a relationship—somehow, the two started to talk about marriage.

Fancy locked lips with her man and they kissed fervently. Her thirst for him was marked by her longing kiss. "I missed you, baby, so much," she uttered ardently, caressing his thick chest.

"I missed you, too," Nasir returned.

Fancy yearned to feel her man inside of her—her sexuality was being awakened by just his presence and touch alone. Her nipples hardened and her pussy throbbed.

She wanted him. She wanted her lover and didn't want to share him with anyone. She didn't want to question his fidelity any longer. Fancy only wanted to suck his dick like no other woman had ever done. She wanted to please her king, lick every inch, and swallow him whole with spit running down her chin and his balls. Fancy wanted to become his freak and lick his nuts and feel them rolling around on her tongue.

It was the intimacy that she missed so much from Nasir. Fancy wanted Nasir to pump his sperm deep inside of her; she was ready to have his baby.

Fancy felt his masculine fingers parting her moistened pussy lips, exposing her hardened clit. His fingers thrust inside of her, between her legs wet with passion. She cooed from the sensation.

"Damn, baby. Ooooh, I want you so bad."

She was heavily aroused, her warm pink lips pulsating. There was no greater pleasure than feeling her lover pleasuring her pussy and her nipples simultaneously—licking them softly and sending delightful sensations directly to her clit. Fancy felt his tongue gently flicking her hardened brown peaks, as he cupped her full breasts to his mouth, back and forth with kisses and the tongue action.

He fingered her gently. Fancy hiked up her skirt much more and was ready to ride his big, black dick in the front seat. Nasir unbuckled his jeans and pulled out his large manhood. He was ready for Fancy to do what she pleased with it. She stroked him lovingly, feeling his hard penis throb in her grip. With her skirt pulled up over her hips and panties pulled off, she slowly straddled him, centering her womanhood toward his mushroom tip, and descended onto his hard erection, giving him access to her treasure. She could feel his width opening up her pink walls. They held each other close and moaned loudly.

Hearing Nasir inhale the scent of sweetness told her that he craved her. Fancy bit her lip, trying to hold back her moans and sounds of pleasure.

"Ooooh, baby, fuck me! Fuck me!"

She tightened her grip around him and grinded her pussy on him, holding him inside of her while trying to make them both come so hard. She panted, feeling his big dick inside of her. Nasir palmed her ass and squeezed, thrusting with vigor. Their sex was intense, causing the car windows to fog up. They fucked deeply until Fancy felt Nasir coming inside of her, and then she came too. Once again, they held onto each other firmly, a bit winded from the powerful sexual encounter. Fancy was high like a kite.

They both needed it.

Nasir stared at the love of his life and said confidently, "Let's do this...let's get married once we deal with this problem. I want you to have my babies."

Fancy waited patiently in the penthouse suite for Jesus to enter the room. She walked over to the floor-to-ceiling windows and looked outside, gazing at Manhattan. With Nasir by her side once again, she felt thankful. They were a team—also engaged and now ready to become one to rule with authority.

Fancy still refused to see her mother in the federal prison, harboring ill feelings toward her and ignoring what both Brenda and Nasir felt was best. Instead, she had to go meet with her father and tell him what was going on.

"It's good to see you again, Rojo," Jesus greeted her while walking into the room with a smile. "I'm glad you could make it once again."

"It's always a pleasure to come and talk with you, Mr. Negro. You have done a lot for me, and I'm much appreciative of everything that you've done," Fancy replied with a smile also. "But we need to talk."

"Of course, like always," Jesus said. "You're like a daughter to me."

Fancy was stunned by his response. She quickly had forgotten what she was about to tell him when he mentioned the word daughter. "A daughter?" she replied, entrenched by his words.

"Yes, a daughter, Rojo," Jesus replied, approaching Fancy closer and staring at her contently. What kind of game was he playing?

"I had children . . . beautiful daughters of my own, and you are as lovely and beautiful as they were once," he added.

Fancy was ready to say, "But we both know that I am your daughter, too," but held her tongue. It disturbed her that Jesus didn't acknowledge her like she was his daughter. Did he love his other two daughters more?

"Were?"

Jesus walked to the window and said, "Yes, were. They were murdered."

"How?" Fancy began to wonder if there was validity in Belen's words.

"The how is not your concern, Fancy. It was the past. Now, we worry and focus on the future."

But he was her future. She was his blood.

"What is it that you have to tell me? You can talk to me about anything. I'm always here for you, Rojo." It was what Alexandro used to say to her when Fancy was young and needed someone to confide in. Jesus seemed to be that shoulder she could lean on for support—but was it all fake?

But now wasn't the time to hash out family ties. She felt a threat brewing, and she didn't know where it was coming from, and how big it was. Fancy had a strong feeling that Pippa was the start of it.

"I have a problem, and this is something really important. My life was threatened a few days ago," she mentioned.

"By who?" Jesus asked.

"I met a woman several months ago, and I don't know what to do.

She came into my world and suddenly betrayed me," Fancy continued. "The other night I think she wanted me dead."

"This woman, who is she? What is her name? You need to give me as much information on the threat, Rojo, and I will take care of it. I promise you this," Jesus replied anxiously.

"Her name is Pippa, or it's the name she has given me. She's from Miami, and we started doing business together. "

"What kind of business?" asked Jesus.

"I became a distributor for her. She was purchasing kilos from me."

"What does she look like?"

Fancy began, "She's older than me. Latina. Late thirties, I think. She has long, black hair and said she's from Miami..."

The questions were pouring in from Jesus' mouth faster than she could answer them. Jesus eyed her intently. He poured himself a quick shot of vodka and was ready to interrogate Fancy intensely.

Fancy had never seen Jesus anxious about anything, but he seemed eager to know everything about Pippa or whoever she was. She gave him Pippa's cell phone number, and any valuable information possible. Fancy then started to think about what her mother had said to her, about her being bait for Jesus to lure in the people that killed his two daughters. It was starting to look like her mother was right after all.

Jesus became very demanding for more information about this new woman that came into Fancy's life.

"Tell me everything about this bitch! I need to know!" Jesus screamed out.

Fancy was shocked by his harsh tone toward her so abruptly. He had transformed into something fear-provoking. He scowled like a lion in the jungle stalking its prey. He wanted to know all the facts about her, and it was getting to the point where he might even threaten Fancy with harm if she didn't give the correct information. Fancy grew tired of the betrayal, deceit, and lies, from her parents, from Pippa, and now Jesus. The puzzle started to come together for her—Belen was right. The only reason Jesus gave her such a strong opportunity in his organization, because he wanted the lie to be believable. It all made sense.

While Jesus was plotting to find this Pippa, Fancy stood in front of him feeling the need to break down. She felt used and detested by him. Jesus was up in arms about this newfound information and about Fancy having a lack of knowledge about the woman. She gave him everything she knew, but to Jesus, it wasn't enough.

Fancy stared at Jesus and it suddenly poured out of her, "Did you ever love me?"

"Did I what?" Jesus replied.

"I'm your daughter, but you used me to find the killers of your other two daughters. You set me up, put me in danger. Why?" Fancy painfully asked.

Jesus remained stoic while Fancy was about to erupt with tears. Even though he wasn't her real father, she missed her Alexandro. His love was genuine and caring. Jesus was a selfish bastard—a monster.

"I gave you everything—power, wealth, respect. I brought you under my wing, and treated you well. I made you," said Jesus with heartiness.

"You used me!" Fancy exclaimed.

"I use everybody. That's fuckin' life, that's how I rise, that's power," Jesus countered.

"I'm not to be used. I'm my own woman."

"You really think that, little girl? You think you have power? With the snap of my fingers I can take everything away from you within a heartbeat. Your mother, dead. Your boyfriend, butchered, and you, you I can keep as a toy," Jesus said coldly.

"I'm no toy. And I'm no girl," Fancy retorted.

Jesus chuckled, "You are my child."

It was the first time Jesus spoke it. But hearing it now just didn't feel right for Fancy. This arrangement wasn't what she expected. She was ready to leave from his sight and depart from the cartel. But it wouldn't be that easy.

"I know everything about you, Jesus," Fancy replied boldly. She refused to use code names any longer. Fuck it—she refused to be scared of Jesus or his cartel.

"What do you know about me? Yes, you have my blood, but you will never be my daughter. I spared your mother long ago when I heard of the news. I could have destroyed you before you were even born, but I didn't," he proclaimed.

"Why didn't you?" Fancy asked with a few tears streaming down her cheeks.

"Your mother was good business. I let her live and carry you for nine months because she was profitable to me at the time. She was a very smart woman, ruthless in her own way. She thinks I kept her alive because she made a vow to keep you a secret. I didn't give a fuck about the pregnancy," he said.

"Did you ever love her?"

"She was a beautiful woman . . . at one time, I did," he admitted.

Fancy became emotional. The tears fell and her heart became heavy. Finally, the truth was out, but she was far from out of the frying pan. It was still hot in the kitchen. And there was still a threat out there, a force that was killing anything connected to Jesus. Fancy was in the crossfire.

"You need to go. You did your part, now let me do mine," Jesus said. "Now go."

Fancy gazed at him with utter disgust. The coldness in his eyes was black like coal, and his tone no longer seemed welcoming or sincere. Jesus turned his back on Fancy and walked toward the window. Fancy lingered in his presence, drying the tears from her face. Where did they go from here? she asked herself.

"I said go!" Jesus reiterated with starkness in his pitch.

"I won't be a fuckin' burden to you anymore," Fancy spat back.

She pivoted on her heels and hurried toward the doorway. Jesus didn't even turn around to see his own daughter leave. His attentiveness was out the window with his arms folded behind him, thinking about his next move on the chessboard. He remained unemotional while Fancy tried to keep her composure and nerves.

CHAPTER 21

Fancy sat in the visiting room of the MDC federal prison, quiet and a little more humble than she'd been during her last visit with her mother. She couldn't believe that she was back again after everything that happened during her last visit. She had vowed to never visit her mother again and insisted that Belen was dead to her—but now, things had changed drastically.

Fancy sat meekly watching Belen approach her with a heavy frown. Her mother had the right to be upset; she was attacked by her own daughter. And Fancy had refused to believe anything she was trying to tell her about Jesus. Now Fancy believed and needed her mother's guidance. She was surprised that Belen hadn't turned down the visit. Maybe all was forgiven. Fancy sat trying to hold it all together, in anguish over the guilt she felt. The emotions were hanging over her like a cloud. Fancy took a deep breath, held back the tears and carried a soft, but apologetic look, watching Belen come near.

"I thought I would never see you again," said Belen, taking a seat opposite Fancy.

The first words coming out of Fancy's mouth were, "I'm sorry, Mommy. I had no right to get upset and put my hands on you. I was just so hurt about everything."

"Ya ass lucky those guards dragged me off you, 'cuz the whipping I was gonna put on you would have left your ass broken up. But you're my daughter and I still love you very much, Fancy," Belen replied from the bottom of her heart.

"I know. And I'm sorry."

"But what brings you here, though? You didn't come here to just apologize to me. Something's going on," Belen said, wisely

"You're right, something is going on. I think my life was threatened the other day."

"Threatened? By who?"

"I fucked up, Mommy. I befriended this woman and let her into my life And I somewhat trusted her and she betrayed me. She and another female tried to come at me in the mall parking lot."

"Fancy, I told you that you can't trust anyone. Everything is business, and there is no such thing as friends in this world we live in," Belen declared.

Fancy nodded.

"Who is she?"

"Her name is Pippa, but I'm for sure that isn't her real name. I had my peoples look strongly into her background to make sure she wasn't a cop and that she was who she said she was," Fancy said.

"So what happened? How did you fuck up?"

"I don't know; everything about her came back legit. I had some of the best hackers investigating her information," Fancy explained.

"But what did your instincts tell you?"

"I think I rushed things with her too quickly, Mommy. I got greedy."

"You got sloppy," Belen chimed.

Fancy held her head down in shame. Her mother was right. Nasir was right also: She had been blinded, and it had almost cost her, her life.

"Who do you think she's connected to?" asked Belen.

"I don't know. She's from Miami."

"You think she's connected to Jesus' peoples?" Belen inquired, eager to hear something.

"She's not. When I went to Jesus to tell him about everything, giving him the information on Pippa, he got excited about it. I've never seen Jesus get wound up like that."

"Hold on. What do you mean he got excited? Like how?" Belen asked with a raised brow and a high-pitched tone.

"I mean, he was excited, super eager to help me and almost threatening me if I didn't come up with the right information to aid him with whatever. I told him everything, Mommy. I just had to let him know," Fancy said.

"Jesus doesn't get excited. I've known this man for many years, and he has always been meticulous and a man of no emotion—stoic. He has mastered that."

Fancy was confused. What was her mother getting at?

"Fancy, the man you've been going to meet, describe him to me," Belen asked.

"He's about five-seven with a muscular build, olive-skinned, with short salt-and-pepper hair. And he's very distinguished and handsome," Fancy described him to a T.

To her mother, the description sounded like Jesus, but she wasn't sure. It also sounded like another Spanish man in the Colombian cartel. Belen had to think for a minute.

"What's going on?" Fancy asked, looking a little worried.

"Let me think," Belen replied, tapping her fingers against the table. Something wasn't right, and she had to decipher the situation.

"Let me ask you a question, Fancy. The man you've been going to see, is he always seated or has he been walking around?"

What kind of question was that? Fancy asked herself. But she answered, "He's been walking around to greet me on several occasions."

"Does he walk with a limp?"

Fancy started to worry. The color was slowly draining from her face. She looked at her mother with concern and replied, "No, he doesn't. He walks around just fine."

Belen looked like she had seen a ghost. Her daughter and been bamboozled and lied to. What game were Jesus and the cartel playing? The expression on Belen's face went from concern to anger. She took her daughter by the hands and looked at her closely. "He is not Jesus."

Fancy's heart dropped. "What? What are you talking about? You can't be fuckin' serious!" Fancy spat.

It felt like she had landed in Oz, or in the Matrix, where nothing was real anymore. Fancy wanted to pinch herself and wake up. The man she believed was her biological father wasn't even Jesus—everything had been fabricated, and for what reason?

"Fancy, let me explain. Jesus walks with a limp and a cane. In the mid-eighties, he was shot several times in the back and barely survived the hit on his life. But one bullet shattered his Achilles heel and he's been walking with a limp for decades," Belen told her.

Fancy was ready to shed tears. This was her breaking point. Once again, she had been lied to and played for a fool. She balled her fists and was ready to go ham realizing that the man she'd been meeting and confiding in, even hugged like he was her daddy, wasn't. He was meant to impersonate Jesus and he did a really good job of it. She was used as bait—but why her?

"I'm sick of this shit," Fancy griped.

"You have to keep strong, Fancy. Now is not the time to lose it, because I need you to be more focused than ever right now," Belen told her.

Seething with rage and emotion, Fancy was ready to implode. They gave her power, but she refused to be controlled and used by them. But how could she go against a cartel? She was only one woman with a crazy boyfriend.

"What should I do?" Fancy asked.

"You fight, Fancy. You let everyone know that you're not just a pawn on the chessboard. You're the queen, and the queen moves any and every way she pleases with no limitations. That's what you are, Fancy, a fuckin' queen," Belen stated with fervor.

Fancy nodded.

It was the first civil talk Fancy had had with her mother in a long while. She took a deep breath and had the urge to give her mother a strong hug. Belen was right. It was time to fight and not look weak.

"Don't let them continue to play my daughter any longer. You fight these muthafuckas, Fancy, and show them who's truly a boss bitch. And if you have to, bide your time, assemble your own crew, and kill 'em all," Belen declared.

CHAPTER 22

It was a joyous day for Fancy and Nasir—something they hadn't felt in a while. The sweet-sixteen birthday party for Nasir's little sister, Lisa, was a direct contrast to their usual hostile environment—the drugs, the murders, the deceit, and the betrayal. They were able to smile and laugh and enjoy the true meaning of life through a youngster's eyes. Nasir and Fancy went all out, dropping a whopping $50,000 for the beautiful young girl on her birthday.

The stylish venue where they held the lavish birthday party cost a pretty penny, but it was well worth it. Lisa brought in her sixteenth birthday like an A-list celebrity. She had dozens of her high-school friends praising her and enjoying the perks that money could buy, from the stylish decorations, $2,000 birthday cake, high-end catering with a chocolate fountain, and a mammoth ice sculpture with an intricate carving that displayed "Happy Birthday, Lisa." A fruit tower display and balloons brought a colorful element to the buffet, and video monitors showed Lisa in her finest moments. It was an all-star event.

Fancy smiled and watched her little cousin parade around the venue. Lisa's sexy blue dress, her long black hair weave flowing down to her back, and the blue heels she wore, made the birthday girl feel like an A-list princess. She was beautiful. It was her day, and Fancy was proud to pay the entire tab. Fancy remembered her own sweet-sixteen birthday party not too long ago. Alexandro had dropped $200,000 for her party, which included a brand-new white Range Rover with a red bow wrapped around the hood.

The DJ had Lil Wayne and Drake blaring in the place, and the teenagers bumped and grinded on the dance floor. Two-hundred-plus people showed up to wish Lisa a happy birthday and revel in the moment of grandeur displayed from wall-to-wall.

Fancy danced gingerly to the beat with a drink in her hand and her eyes on her little cousin who was parading around the venue with a large smile on her face. It brought Fancy back to a time when she was that young—an innocent, spoiled, little princess being showered with gifts and love. She fixed her eyes on Lisa and smiled. For a moment, her mind had been taken off of the violence and drama in her life. Tonight, it was about fun and family.

Brenda was mingling with the adults at the party—or more like flirting with the handsome males—in her tight jeans and sexy top. Brenda was an image of Fancy's mother, but she had seen harder times in her life while living in Brooklyn. Over time, Fancy grew to love and respect Brenda. She was real and abrasive, but underneath it all, Brenda was a nice woman with a heart of gold.

"She looks beautiful tonight," Nasir said, flanking Fancy with a smile of his own.

"Yes, she does." Fancy slid into the arms of her man and nestled against him lovingly.

Nasir stared at his beautiful little sister, who was becoming a woman. This was a moment in his life that he would always cherish. The fact that they were able to afford to give Lisa the best birthday party ever made the violent lifestyle that they chose to live all worth it. Nasir's family didn't have to struggle any longer. They weren't born with silver spoons in their mouths like Fancy, but they all had risen from the bottom to the top. From Al-Saadiq to the twins, life was a blessing.

"Any word from your peoples on that bitch Pippa?" Nasir asked, deciding to talk business during a time of pleasure.

"Not yet, but everyone's on it."

"What we need to do is take a trip down to Miami and hunt that bitch down. I got peoples down there that can help us out," Nasir said.

Fancy thought about it. But it was risky, because they would be in Pippa's territory. She was out there somewhere, and danger could come from any direction. Fancy and Nasir weren't fools, though; security was tight, but very subtle at Lisa's birthday party. They didn't want to scare the teens and their parents with henchmen armed with machine guns and automatic weapons. So the men moved through the venue dressed in black suits and shoes, with their weapons holstered underneath their jackets and looking like Secret Service agents.

It gave Fancy some comfort to see them around. She wasn't strapped, but in her car were a few weapons that would come in handy if anyone tried her tonight on their ride home. But tonight was all fun. Fancy gazed at Nasir—it was the first time she ever seen her man in a black-and-white Kenneth Cole suit and shoes. Fancy eyed Nasir with admiration. He was so handsome.

"You look good, baby," she said.

"And you look gorgeous, Fancy. You are so beautiful, baby," Nasir replied.

"You care to dance?"

"I don't dance," he replied.

"Just this once, enjoy the night and relax," Fancy said with a warm smile.

She took Nasir by the hand and started leading him toward the dance floor, where everyone was cutting a rug and enjoying a wonderful party.

KIM K.

The place was dimmed with disco lights dancing everywhere, jazzing up the floor. The DJ put on "Electric Boogie," and the party guests went berserk. Immediately the dance floor became crowded with everyone doing the fall wall line dance set to the Marcia Griffiths song.

Fancy and Nasir joined in the line dance. Fancy was on point, moving and flowing with the crowd with the happiest smile on her face. She moved next to her cousin Lisa, and the rhythm flowed through both of them like a current.

"I see you doin' your thang, cousin," Lisa said ecstatically.

"Girl, you can't keep up with me." Fancy messed about, sliding and gliding and turning with the others.

Nasir seemed a little lost at first, trying to keep up with everyone else, but he soon got the hang of it and was on cue. He joined Fancy and his sister gliding and sliding across the floor like they were on ice. Even Brenda, the twins, and Al-Saadiq joined in on the fun. For once, they all felt like one big happy family.

The DJ was mixing and cutting R&B and hip-hop effortlessly and had the party jumping. Fancy started to break out into a sweat as she danced with Lisa from song to song—reggae, R&B, and rap. For almost an hour, she partied hard with her family. And then before 11pm, they wanted to wish Lisa a happy sweet-sixteenth birthday and have her open up all of her gifts that were neatly placed on the long table near the pricey birthday cake.

The DJ lowered the blaring music so Brenda was able to get on the microphone and address the crowd. Brenda stood on the platform with a smile aimed at her daughter below her and said, "Happy sixteenth birthday, baby girl. You are so beautiful and I'm so proud of you. This is your night, and to be sixteen years old is such a blessing. I remember when I turned sixteen five years ago . . ."

The crowd laughed.

"Don't you mean a hundred years ago?" Nasir joked.

The crowd erupted with louder laughter.

Brenda shot her son a fixed stare and then continued, "Like I was sayin', when I turned sixteen a few years ago, it was nothing like this. You deserve this, baby girl. You're an A student and you never give Mommy any trouble."

Brenda then turned to look at Fancy and Nasir. She smiled. She then said to them, "And I want to thank my son and Fancy for arranging everything for my daughter. I love y'all."

"We love you, too, Aunt Brenda," Fancy shouted.

"Okay, enough of this sappy shit, let's open some gifts, eat some expensive cake, and party until we drop," Brenda hollered, shaking her hips and getting excited.

Everyone went over to the gifts and cake. There was a decorated chair for Lisa to sit in where she would be able to open up all of her gifts in comfort.

First came the cutting of her extraordinary birthday cake. It was a stunning, towering chocolate and vanilla cake that was designed to look like Hogwarts School of Witchcraft and Wizardry from the Harry Potter movie series. It was Lisa's favorite story. Everyone started taking pictures of the intricate cake with their camera phones.

"Ohmygod!" Lisa uttered in awe. "I love it!"

"We all know how much you loved Harry Potter, so we decided you should have your own castle," Fancy said.

She loved it and loved it some more. The cake looked so lovely and real that she didn't want to cut into it. But her guests all wanted a piece of the castle. The candles were lit and everyone surrounded Lisa and sang "Happy Birthday" to her in unison.

Afterwards, it was time for the gift opening. Nasir watched his little sister unwrap all her gifts with cheer and laughter. His gift to her was a diamond locket with a small picture inside of him and her taken a few years back when they went to Coney Island. Lisa always said it was her favorite picture of them. When Lisa saw it, she beamed with joy, jumped from her chair, and hugged her brother tightly.

"Thank you, Nasir," she said with joy.

"Only the best for my baby sister."

Fancy had gotten her a pair of diamond earrings and her own pair of Jimmy Choos that cost $1,500—diamonds were always a girl's best friend, and a pair of stylish shoes were a woman's pleasure. Lisa was ecstatic.

After opening countless gifts from family and friends, and a night of fun, the party started to wind down after midnight. Almost everyone was exhausted from having so much fun and eating like pigs from the high-end catering. Nasir and Fancy retreated to the outside to get some fresh air and smoke a cigarette. Tomorrow, they all planned on going to Splish Splash for an afternoon of more fun. The weekend was going to be one unforgettable one.

Brenda exited the venue carrying both twins in her arms. They were sleeping and ready to hit the bed. Al-Saadiq was behind them, wide awake and still live like a wire. He didn't want to go home just yet. He wanted to hang out with his big brother.

"Ma, I don't wanna leave yet. I wanna ride wit' Nasir," he said.

"Boy, bring ya ass on here and get in the damn car. Nasir got things to do and he ain't trying to be bothered wit' you," Brenda fussed.

Al-Saadiq pursed his lips and began to pout. He was fifteen and wanted to be treated like a man. He glared at his mother and spat, "Ma, I'm fifteen now, so stop treatin' me like I'm a kid. I'm grown like Nasir!"

Brenda pivoted in his direction, shot a hard stare at her defiant son, and retorted, "Al-Saadiq, I ain't got time for ya fuckin' bullshit, boy. I'm ya ride home unless you ready to walk ya ass back to Brooklyn. Now come on now!"

Al-Saadiq sucked his teeth and sighed heavily. It looked like a standoff between the two of them. Brenda was ready to snatch her son by the neck and drag him to the car. Nasir chimed, "Ma, it's cool. I got him. He can ride back wit' me."

"You sure, Nasir?" Brenda asked.

"He's my little brother. He's in good hands. I got him," Nasir assured her. Brenda looked reluctant at first. Nasir changed her mind when he said, "I won't keep him out late. Let me talk to him. I haven't had a chat wit' him in a minute."

"Remember, he's fifteen, Nasir, and I don't want him around any of your hoodlums. He's a good kid."

"I'll only have him around my hoes," Nasir joked.

Al-Saadiq smiled widely.

"Ha-ha, ya funny, Nasir," Brenda replied dryly.

"She be actin' like I'm a virgin," Al-Saadiq slyly said under his breath.

"What the fuck you said, boy?" Brenda exclaimed.

"I didn't say anything, Ma," Al-Saadiq meekly replied.

"I thought so."

Nasir laughed. "Damn, you let her punk you like that?"

"Nasir, shut the fuck up and leave him alone and stop instigating shit. You about to get that boy fucked up out here!" Brenda hollered.

Fancy stood on the sidelines, watching the entertainment. It was quite amusing to her to see family joke around. Her mind was temporarily free from any worry. It was a beautiful night with humor and fun, and everyone wanted to enjoy every minute of it. Brenda climbed into the spanking new Yukon Nasir had bought her and she gave both her sons a stern warning. "I ain't playin' wit' y'all. Don't get into any shit out there, cuz I'll beat both y'all asses."

Nasir, Al-Saadiq, and Fancy climbed into the pearl-white Range Rover and were ready to head into the bustling Manhattan on a warm and clear summer night to hang out at one of Fancy's favorite nightspots. It didn't matter that Al-Saadiq was underage. Money talked, and the two had some heavy influences in the city for Al-Saadiq to have a really good time and have him party like a rock star.

Nasir lingered behind the wheel of the Range Rover, watching his mother drive off. Fancy was riding shotgun and Al-Saadiq sat in the backseat behind Fancy. He was all smiles and very appreciative that his big brother looked out for him.

"Where we goin'?" he asked eagerly.

"You just sit back and chill, and don't embarrass me tonight. Ya hear me?" Nasir commanded.

"Yeah, I hear you," Al-Saadiq replied submissively.

Al-Saadiq started to roll up a blunt. The couple didn't mind; they too were ready to smoke and get high off some kush. The engine to the Range Rover purred nicely. The radio was playing Drake and Nicki Minaj. It was about to a really fun night—so they thought.

Al-Saadiq took a few pulls from the burning blunt and said to Nasir as he was passing it, "Damn, this some good shit. Bro, you gonna love it."

As Nasir reached for the blunt, suddenly a dark-colored truck came to a screeching stop on the passenger side, and before the occupants in the Range could realize what was going on, several semi-automatic weapons abruptly emerged from the windows and opened fire.

Bak! Bak! Bak! Bak!

Boom! Boom! Boom!

Gunfire exploded like firecrackers going off, and several rounds tore into the front and back passenger doors. Fancy screamed and quickly ducked down into her seat, reaching for the .9mm near her grasp. But she was too inundated with extreme gunfire to retaliate. The passenger window shattered, and shards of glass fell on top of her. Chaos ensued in public and people scattered for cover hurriedly. Nasir rapidly ejected himself from behind the wheel, stumbling to the ground with shots tearing into his ride. He pulled out his pistol, screaming, "Muthafuckas!"

"Nasir! Nasir!" Fancy screamed frantically.

Crouching low and rushing to the back of his truck to counter attack, Nasir sprang into action. He fired his Glock17 in a frenzy at the dark truck and shattered the back glass, rounds penetrating everywhere. Scowling heavily with his arm outstretched and the gun at the end of it, he boldly charged forward, firing rapidly at his attackers. Gunshots echoed into the night wildly. The truck started to race off, tires screeching and shots ringing out, and Nasir chased behind it. The truck roared down the road and made a sharp right, fading from his view.

Nasir stood in the middle of the street fuming with the gun down at his side. He wanted to scream.

"Ohmygod . . . Nasir!" he heard Fancy scream out.

Nasir turned and ran toward her screaming. When he got to the bullet-riddled Range Rover, Fancy didn't have a scratch on her, but Al-Saadiq wasn't so lucky. He was slumped over in the seat, shot three times, and they didn't know how severe it was. Nasir snatched open the back door and pulled his little brother into his arms.

"Al-Saadiq, c'mon, get up! Don't do this to me! Get the fuck up!" Nasir screamed out with tears beginning to well up in his eyes.

He shook his brother's listless body, repeatedly trying to get a reaction, but there was no response at all. Fancy began to cry. Blood coated the seats and Al-Saadiq. A crowd started to form around the truck. Shocked and worried faces gazed at a furious Nasir.

"We need to get him to a hospital," Fancy cried out.

But Nasir's gut told him that his little brother was dead. They didn't need a hospital—they didn't need anything but the morgue. And the only thing Nasir wanted was revenge. He clenched his fists so tightly that his fingernails broke skin, causing him to bleed a little. His eyes were red with grief and anger. He couldn't hold back the tears any longer and started to weep with his dead brother in his arms.

"I'm gonna fuckin' kill every last one of them," he shouted furiously, still holding onto his brother's limp body.

Nasir didn't know how he was going to explain her son's death it to his mother. His chest tightened and his breathing became sparse. He didn't know who tried to murder them, but he was going to find out and make them wish that they were never born. With a list of enemies to choose from, everyone was at risk, because it was war.

The Brooklyn cemetery was overflowing with family and friends mourning the death of Al-Saadiq. They were all gathered around a twenty-gauge steel casket covered with flowers and roses that was about to be lowered into the earth.

The ominous sky looked like it was about to pour heavy rain onto the burial. But everyone was nestled together under the wide canopy. Nasir stood next to his grieving mother dressed in all black with his eyes covered with dark shades. He gazed at the casket in front of him with a gaping sense of guilt that he couldn't protect his little brother.

When Brenda first heard the news of Al-Saadiq's death, she let out a blood curling scream and collapsed. Then she went and attacked Nasir, banging her balled fists against his chest, crying profusely, and blaming him for her son's death.

"You said you were goin' to look out for him! You were supposed to protect him! Why? Why?" She had cried out with such a strong grief that she looked inconsolable.

Nasir had pulled his mother into his arms and held her tightly. She tried to fight and resist him, but he refused to let her go. The only thing he could do to ease her pain was to avenge Al-Saadiq's death.

For Fancy, the tears couldn't stop trickling from her eyes. It was a miracle that she was still alive after the attempt on their life. She could hear the bullets whizzing by, barely missing her and being covered with shards of glass. Why was she so fortunate to still be breathing and her little cousin wasn't? The gunmen were only after her and Nasir. It was one of those fucked-up coincidences.

She stood next to a stoic Nasir. He hadn't spoken a word or shed a single tear since the funeral had started. Brenda was a wreck; her wailing for her dead son echoed beyond the cemetery. She was dressed in all black with a black veil over her face, and it looked like at any moment she was ready to leap onto her son's casket and be buried along with him.

"Oh my baby, my baby . . . why?" she cried out. "Why him?"

Family held her close and tried to console her while the pastor went on to give the eulogy.

"In the sweat of thy face shalt thou eat bread, till thou return unto the ground; for out of it wast thou taken: for dust thou art, and unto dust shalt thou return. We therefore commit his body to the ground; earth to earth, ashes to ashes, dust to dust . . ." The African American pastor stood behind the casket, draped in a luxurious black divinity robe with hand sewn blue velvet panels and doctoral bars.

After the eulogy, mourners started to toss white roses onto the casket as the caretakers began lowering it into the ground. Brenda released a loud, high-pitched scream and had to be restrained by several friends from jumping onto it.

"My baby! No, not my baby! Take me, oh Lord, take me!" she screamed out with tears streaming from her eyes.

Nasir had seen enough. He walked away from the burial site in anger. He didn't want to see them put his baby brother into the dirt. Fancy followed behind him.

"Nasir!" she called out.

He continued walking, ignoring her completely. His mind was clouded with rage and profound sadness. He proceeded toward the motorcade not too far from the burial. Since the shooting he had been on the phone with his goons and connects trying to find out who were the ones responsible. He fingered the cartel for the hit, but why? Jesus was kind enough to give his condolences to the family and arranged for a large shipment of flowers to be sent to the burial site. Fancy didn't want anything to do with Jesus. She still kept Nasir in the dark about everything that had transpired. But she couldn't keep lying to him any longer.

Then he thought about Pippa. She was definitely a prime suspect, and when they tracked her down he was ready to tear her head off with his bare fuckin' hands. Every single foe of his and Fancy's came into his mind, from Li'l-Un to disgruntled street soldiers. He was ready for war in the New York hoods.

Nasir stood near the motorcade smoking a cigarette. The crowd near the burial site started to disperse and go their separate ways. He watched his mother come his way, escorted by family members, with the tears still falling from her eyes. Flanked by Fancy he heard her say, "Baby, we need to have a talk."

Nasir nodded halfheartedly.

Brenda walked toward her son, wiping away tears. With her eyes fixed on him, she went to reach for Nasir. Brenda stared intensely at her oldest boy and said to him, "You make them pay for this, Nasir. Whoever did this to my son, you make them pay heavily. I want them all dead."

Nasir locked eyes with his mother and nodded. It was a promise he planned on keeping to the fullest. He was ready to kill them all; butcher every last one of them like he'd witnessed the Colombians do to the men in the cabin.

"They're already dead men walkin', Ma."

Brenda climbed into the black limousine feeling disheartened. Friends and family continued to comfort her. He watched the limo drive off with the remainder of his family in it. Nasir, in his own world, decided to walk back over to the gravesite and pay his respects alone. Fancy refused to leave his side, but now she gave Nasir a moment alone. However, they had a lot to talk about. While Nasir spent a half-hour talking and apologizing to Al-Saadiq, she waited patiently with her mind spinning with so much concern.

He said his piece and walked toward Fancy. It was time—no more games.

Nasir gazed at Fancy and asked, "What ya peoples got on this bitch? Cuz we goin' down to Miami and we ain't coming back until this bitch and everything connected to her is dead."

"Jason is already on it and he'll have something for me soon."

"Tell him to hurry it up and find something fast," Nasir said.

"He will. I trust his work."

"So how he fucked up last time? When he supposedly checked out Pippa's credentials?" Nasir asked.

Fancy didn't have a reasonable answer for him. She looked stunned for a moment, and then replied, "He won't miss this time. I guarantee it."

"He better not."

Jason was her computer hacker/tech—a computer whiz since they were at private school together—and he was the one she had gone to, to investigate Pippa. When it came to technology and surveillance, her friend Jason was someone who was able to seek and exploit any weaknesses in a computer system or computer network. He had an advanced understanding of systems and their weaknesses. He was able to duplicate any I.D or paperwork with unbelievable authenticity. He'd first hacked into the school system to change his failing grade into a passing one.

Once Jason came back with valuable information they needed, they were going to Miami to hunt Pippa down. But before they made a serious move like that, Fancy knew she needed to come clean to Nasir about everything. He deserved to know the truth.

The cemetery had cleared out of all mourners and they had their privacy. Another cigarette was lit up by Nasir. The sky had turned completely dark and threatening. It finally started to rain, so the two headed to the burgundy Yukon to talk alone.

As the heavy rain began to cascade off the windshield, pouring down around them, Fancy looked at Nasir and was ready to spill the truth about her relationship with Jesus and the cartel.

Fancy was candid with him. "Jesus is my biological father." It discharged out of her like a live round. She waited for the aftermath.

Nasir, looking confused, replied, "What the fuck are you talkin' about, Fancy?"

"Alexandro was never my real father. I didn't find out from my mother until recently. She just sprung it on me. Jesus asked to meet with me and I leaped at the opportunity."

"And you decided to keep this from me all this time? Why?"

"My mother. She warned me to keep it quiet. She was nervous. She didn't know Jesus' true motive."

"His motive? He gave you keys to a fuckin' empire," Nasir barked.

"And I never took the time to question why," Fancy replied. "And now I know the why."

Nasir, still befuddled, harshly responded, "Your father, all this time . . . Ain't that a bitch? And you spring this shit on me right now, after my brother's murder? So what other secrets you been keepin' from me?"

"I'm sorry, baby," Fancy muttered. "A lot has been going on, and it was hard for me to explain."

Nasir looked at Fancy not telling him the truth as some sort of betrayal. He yelled, "I'm ya fuckin' man, Fancy! Why the fuck you gotta keep me in the dark? I'm lookin' fuckin' crazy right now. The whole damn time!"

Fancy held back the emotions and tears. "There's more."

Nasir didn't know if he was ready to hear more. He'd just buried his little brother, the head of the cartel was Fancy's real father, and now he'd made a promise to kill whoever was responsible for Al-Saadiq's murder and he didn't have a name yet.

"How much more?" he asked heatedly.

Fancy took a deep breath and let it all out. She went on to tell him everything that transpired in the past several months with the cartel and Pippa, breaking down that the man she was meeting wasn't really Jesús but an impostor and how everything was fabricated. She told him about Jesús' two daughters being murdered in Colombia and how Jesús only established business and a relationship with her to use her as bait and lure in the killers of his family.

"What the fuck is this shit, the Twilight Zone?" Nasir uttered. "All this goin' on wit' you, and you couldn't tell me. You don't trust me?"

"I do—"

"It don't fuckin' feel like it!"

"Well I'm telling you now."

With a stern look aimed at Fancy, Nasir asked, "So what now? Are we still in business wit' the cartel, or do I gotta worry about them comin' at me and my family?"

"I'm handling things."

"You handling things, huh. How?" Nasir shouted. "Look around you, Fancy, shit is all fucked up! And I'm gonna be the one to have to fix it. But I'll promise you this, if the cartel come at me or mines then there's gonna be hell to pay. Cuz I ain't gonna be butchered like some fuckin' pig. They gonna have to shoot me down in the fuckin' street."

"You, me, and our family won't be touched, baby. I promise you that," Fancy replied with conviction.

"Why, cuz the queen said so?" Nasir replied, sarcastically. "The queen ain't got reign over shit."

"Fuck you!" Fancy cursed.

"No, fuck you, Fancy! You got into sumthin' that was way over ya head and look what the fuck happened! My little brother is dead now, and you been played for a fuckin' fool," he retorted.

"And I'm the one to blame?! This all my fault, like you're Mary fuckin' Poppins and shit? You're a killer Nasir, with a lot more enemies out there than me."

"And who do I mostly kill for?" he countered.

She was about ready to tell Nasir off and curse him out, and they were about to get into an intense argument until Fancy's cell phone rang. She looked at the caller I.D. and saw it was Jason calling. The phone call somewhat defused the tension in the SUV when she decided to answer.

"What, Jason?" she hollered into the phone.

"Good news, Fancy. I found that sneaky bitch," Jason said.

"Pippa?"

"No, but the friend she was with in New York," he explained.

"How the fuck did you find her?"

"I'm the master of this shit, Fancy. They don't call me The Wizard for no reason. But I remember the time and location you gave me about the incident in Green Acres Mall, and I used the video surveillance in the area to search out any Audi S8s that were around, especially the one they were in. You already gave me the color, so it was somewhat easier to track, but it was still tedious work. It took a few days to pinpoint the right car and model, but I found it. Then I ran the plates, used video recognition from the surveillance footage available, and processed the gathered information through my system that I designed. The car was rented from a privileged Manhattan exotic car dealership/rental on the West Side called Gotham Dream Cars," Jason proclaimed proudly.

"The Wizard strikes again!"

"But there's more," Jason continued. "And you're going to love this, Fancy. I ran everything. Of course that criminal bitch had priors. They call her "Sexy," but her real name is Maria Johnson. She's from Brooklyn, New York, but resides in Miami. She was released a year ago from MCC prison, and she got a list of charges from attempted murder, robbery, fraud, extortion, kidnapping, and so on. She's a dangerous bitch, Fancy," Jason warned.

"And what am I, not dangerous?" she countered. "But enough of the bullshit, give me what I need, Jason."

"Your wish is my command, my queen," he messed about. "She stays a high-rise building on Brickell Avenue."

"I owe you, Jason," Fancy said with a smile.

"You'll get my bill in the mail. And I'm expensive. But you already know," Jason gleefully replied. "Oh, and I pulled a picture of her from the New York DMW. I'll send that as well."

"I already know what she looks like but send it anyway."

"Done. I always got you."

She hung up and was ready to share the good news with Nasir.

"What he had to say?" Nasir asked hoarsely with a frown.

"We're going to Miami. He found one of them," she told him.

CHAPTER 23

M iami, with its turquoise water and sandy beaches was an attractive city. Fancy had seen the city numerous times, but it was Nasir's first time in Miami. He wasn't impressed. He didn't care for the beaches, exotic clubs, or warm weather. His main focus was revenge. Just like his trip to Greenville, South Carolina, he wanted to hunt the bitches down, kill them slowly, and head back to New York. He didn't want to stay in Miami any longer than needed.

It was dusk, and the atmosphere was warm and quiet on Brickell Avenue. Nasir watched the entrance to the towering high rise like a hawk. He, Fancy, and Ozone sat parked across the street from the place in a rented Impala. It was something inconspicuous and easy to drive around the city with the navigational system attached on the dashboard. The three occupants were heavily armed and impatient.

As soon as their flight had landed at Miami International Airport in the early evening, Fancy was on the phone calling her connection in the area so they would have quick access to guns, a car, and information. When they walked out of the terminal, they were greeted by Donovan, an old friend of Alexandro's. He was one of the few that stood by her family's side when the indictments were handed out and arrests were made.

Donovan was a dark-skinned male who stood six feet tall with a powerful build. He was a businessman first, running a Fortune 500 company in Miami like the shrewd tycoon he was, but he was also a hardcore gangster connected with many high-level mobsters and thugs in the city.

He had greeted Fancy and her men outside the terminal dressed to the nines in a white and gray pinstripe Armani suit with his dark blue, four-door Bentley idling outside.

The three had climbed into the Bentley and were welcomed to champagne, drinks, and caviar. They drove in the direction of the city and Donovan was ready to make Fancy and her two guests feel like they were home. Introductions were made, and then it was about business.

"I suppose I can't change your mind about what you're planning to do," Donovan said to her.

"No you can't, Donovan. We came down here for a reason."

"Fancy, why don't you let me handle this, because I owe it to you and your father, and you and your friends can get back on the plane without any worries? I can call up a few professionals to handle two simple ladies."

"This is personal, and I want my face to be the last face she ever sees on this earth when I slowly cut her throat," she replied.

"I see. Well then, I've made all the proper arrangements from guns to a decent car service, and you'll be well provided for and taking care of."

"Thank you, Donovan," Fancy returned, grateful.

Fancy felt she was in good hands with her father's old friend of over twenty years. And being true to his word, he armed Fancy and her goons with several automatic weapons and a comfortable, low-key car to get around in. Donovan had done his part as promised, and now it was time for Fancy and Nasir to do theirs.

It didn't take long for them to find the high-rise on Brickell. Using the information Jason had given them, they studied the picture of Sexy.

He'd also sent a few locations of where she might be and was aware of the car she drove—a tricked-out Chrysler 300 with 20-inch chromed rims and vertical doors. It was definitely easy to spot on the streets.

The trio waited patiently on the block, chain smoking, checking weapons, and cracking jokes. Two hours went by and the area was still. It was an affluent area where money and luxury talked and the poor kept on walking by.

Ozone took a few pulls from a Newport and exhaled. He was itching for some excitement. "Where is this fuckin' bitch?" he asked. He was bloodthirsty like a vampire and couldn't wait to use his specialized toys on someone. He didn't care who. He was a scary-looking man with war scars and bad teeth.

"Y'all sure ya got da right place?" he asked.

"We sure," Nasir replied.

It was completely dark. Another two hours had gone by, and now the three were completely restless. They had been parked and waiting on the block for too long now and Fancy didn't want to bring any suspicion on themselves. Fancy made the decision to leave. Nasir was against it. He didn't care how long they had to wait; he just wanted to avenge his little brother's death. But Fancy figured there were other ways to find Sexy or their main course, Pippa.

Fancy knew it wasn't her real name, and she yearned to find out everything about her before she died. Who sent her and why? Was she working alone? One way or the other, Fancy was going to get what she came for.

"Nasir, we can't sit out here all night. We going to look crazy," said Fancy as she started up the car.

"Then where you tryin' to go?" Nasir asked.

"Food and some rest. We can't starve ourselves looking for these bitches."

"Fuck it then, let's go."

Fancy maneuvered the Impala off the block and headed toward the nearest highway. Today had been unsuccessful, but it was okay, because they weren't leaving the city until they all had blood on their hands.

The following two nights it was the same routine—on the hunt, but no results. Fancy hoped the information she received from Jason was on point. But it seemed like the place had been emptied out. Fancy hoped the bitches weren't tipped off to their arrival.

The three cruised around South Beach, taking in the attractive scenery. As Fancy drove, she received a surprise phone call. The number was anonymous. When she answered, the first thing Fancy heard was, "I heard you're looking for someone named Sexy." It was a male voice.

"Who is this?" Fancy demanded.

"Let's just say I'm a friend of a friend. And the information I'm about to tell you doesn't come cheap."

"And how do I know you're legit? And how the fuck did you get this number?"

"You don't, but what I'm about to tell you is one-hundred."

"How much?"

"I want two hundred thousand."

"What?"

"I know you can afford it, Fancy. And I know how much you want Pippa," he said.

Hearing him bring up Pippa's name made Fancy realize he could be telling the truth. But it truly bothered her that she didn't know who the caller was. It could also be a setup. Nasir and Ozone became aware of the conversation going on. They kept quiet and let Fancy do the talking.

"So how do we make this arrangement?" Fancy asked.

"I'll call you back in an hour with the details," he said.

Before he hung up, Fancy was able to say, "And to let you know, I have very powerful friends everywhere, and if this information I'm paying for isn't legit, then I can guarantee you won't be anonymous for long. And they'll start finding pieces of you everywhere for the next year."

"I guarantee you, Fancy, the information is legitimate. I want that bitch dead too. Like I said, I'll call back in an hour to give you the details."

The caller hung up. Nasir was curious about the call. She filled him in with the details. But the one issue was the two hundred thousand. Even though she was worth millions, coming up with two hundred thousand dollars within a short time wasn't that simple when she was in a different city. She had to call in one more favor.

She decided to call Donovan. When he answered, the first thing out of Fancy's mouth was, "I need you again. I have a huge favor to ask you."

He was listening.

Fancy told him her situation and asked him for some advice. She didn't know this caller, or his motive, but he was giving her a rare opportunity. They had searched all through Miami looking for Sexy and Pippa, and even with all the information they had on them, the women were impossible to find.

Donovan agreed to front Fancy the two hundred thousand, knowing she was good for it.

With South Beach buzzing with night life and city activity from corner to corner, Fancy thought about a different chapter in her life when she was a spoiled teenager spending her daddy's money, staying in five-star hotels, eating lobster and shrimp almost every night, and going on thousand-dollar shopping sprees. It was a time when she was rich, but innocent. Now, she was richer, but her innocence was a mere memory.

It didn't take long for Donovan to send one of his trusted associates with the two hundred thousand in a small duffel bag. The drop-off was discreet, in a parking garage that Donovan's company owned. Once she had the money it also didn't take long for her to receive the phone call from the anonymous male.

Fancy assured him that she had the cash for the information.

"Are you familiar with South Beach?" he asked.

"I am."

"Then meet me at the Balans café on Ocean Drive in a half-hour."

"We'll be there."

Fancy had to be cautious and smart. Not knowing the face of the man she was talking to and giving him two hundred thousand dollars was a very risky move. But they wanted Pippa and Sexy so bad.

"You trust this, Fancy?" Nasir asked.

"Right now, we don't have a choice."

Balans, on Ocean Drive, was a quintessential South Beach café in the middle of the action, complete with sunny-colored, oversized umbrellas— the perfect place for brunch or a light dinner. Inside, it was a beautifully renovated classic Deco building featuring a beautiful (though small) staircase reminiscent of the 1940s and a small bar that invited you to have a seat as soon as you walked through the door.

Fancy and Nasir walked into the establishment while Ozone stood watch by the car. The anonymous caller chose to meet in public because it was less risk for him. With hordes of people and a steady patrol of cops, someone would be stupid to try and pull off something there.

Fancy and Nasir walked toward the bar where they were told he would find them. They were at the bar no less than five minutes when Fancy heard, "You have the money with you?"

But it wasn't a male asking her; it was a young woman who looked to be in her late teens or early twenties. Fancy and Nasir were shocked.

The girl read their look and quickly replied, "Don't judge me, cuz y'all far from know me."

"I'm not judging, but who are you?"

"A friend."

"And the male caller?" Fancy wanted to know.

"He's a friend, too. But we both would like to become rich and see Sexy dead," the girl replied. She was posh with her words and she seemed to be educated.

Fancy sized her up; the girl's wardrobe was like her own—sexy but classy. She was light-skinned with green eyes, curves, and long, raven-black hair. She was extremely beautiful. Who was she?

"I know what you're thinking. Who am I really, and why should you trust me?" said the girl.

"You're right. I don't even know your name," Fancy replied.

"Cindy."

"Okay, Cindy. What's your beef with Sexy?"

"Sexy is my sister, and I hate her fucking guts. And as for my male friend that called you, he chooses to remain anonymous. But if you don't trust us, then you can trust our information," Cindy proclaimed.

Nasir only listened; Fancy had the situation by the helm. Sexy's own sister was betraying her. And to make Fancy believe her Cindy said, "My sister loves pussy, and she frequents this gay bar called Twist every weekend in South Beach."

The info seemed legit to Fancy.

Cindy added, "I've given you enough before I got paid. There's more after I get paid."

Fancy nodded to Nasir. He picked up the bag and handed it to Cindy with an intimidating frown, but she wasn't moved by his hard look.

"Spend it in good health," were the only words Nasir said to her.

"I will," she countered with a smirk at him.

With the money in her possession, Cindy became a windfall of information, betraying her sister. She told Fancy everything she needed to know, from recent addresses to favorite hangouts, including the bad history between herself and her sister. Fancy felt a little more comfortable paying her the two hundred thousand.

"Are we done here?" Cindy asked.

Fancy nodded.

"It was nice doing business with you," said Cindy, pivoting to make her exit with the small duffle bag gripped tightly.

"But one thing," Fancy chimed.

Cindy turned around slightly. "And what's that?"

"I'm not to be fucked with," Fancy said with a scowl.

"I know. I heard about you. And I'm only focused on getting paid. Your connection with Donovan speaks volumes."

"As long as we have that understanding," Fancy replied.

Cindy nodded and left Balans discreetly. Fancy and Nasir left behind her, climbing back into the idling Impala with Ozone patiently waiting for them. Fancy was extremely happy with the newfound information she had received from Cindy.

CHAPTER 24

The infamous gay club Twist, in South Beach, was known throughout the world for its great music, friendly staff, and sizeable crowd of hot tourists and locals alike. It was like seven bars in one, with each bar having its own unique atmosphere and decor. The patrons could literally "bar hop" without ever leaving the two-story club.

The place was packed with patrons jamming to punk rock, reggae, and R&B. The blaring music, dimmed lighting, and disco lights were prime time for the gay men and women in the pub, which was the first bar everyone encountered when entering Twist. It artfully combined an English gentleman's club decor with the audio and visual of music videos.

Twist was a magnificent place of entertainment from every square inch of the place—the outside was a quieter "garden" area with plants, mood lighting, and a bar that featured tropical drinks. Outside of the garden was the tiki, a tropical "bungalow bar," which was best known for "Gaiety," a collection of erotic men dancing for your pleasure. Upstairs the ocean breezes flowed through the veranda-style "patio bar," and as the night thickened past midnight, the size of the crowd had grown in equal proportion to its intensity.

The "Main Room" DJ was setting the bass and the beat to the cutting-edge tribal house rhythms, and the club staff were personable and attractive professionals with an understanding of their customers. Sexy was at the center of it all, moving seductively to the blaring music, clad in a revealing white ultralow-cut halter top with open back and gold metallic boy shorts. She was eye-candy in the place, receiving attention from both gay men and women.

She danced heavily, looking like a video vixen in her scanty attire. She was alone on the dance floor for a moment until she caught the attention of a beautiful and exotic long-legged blond female who looked Brazilian. She was a goddess in Sexy's eyes. They caught each other's attention, and with her eyes transfixed on the extraordinary Brazilian beauty, Sexy made her way over to introduce herself. Esmeralda was out of town, so she had time to stray away and play some games.

Approaching with a glinting stare, Sexy hollered over the blaring music, "What is your name?"

The Brazilian blond smiled. "Rochelle." Her accent was authentic and intoxicating.

"I'm Sexy."

"Yes, you are," Rochelle complimented with a flirtatious grin.

"Thanks."

Sexy took the lead during the conversation by pulling Rochelle closer to her, showing her eagerness to touch and maybe fondle a little, if allowed. Rochelle turned her back toward Sexy, displaying her luscious backside and full-figured curves. It was an enticing moment for the both of them. Rochelle's naughty smile aimed at Sexy hinted that later on they might be able to do more than dance with each other.

Twist was swelling out of control with a rapidly growing crowd. But in the middle of it all the two females seemed to be in their own world.

"You are something else, I have to say."

"You gonna talk or you gonna dance with me?" Rochelle replied, shaking her hips to the beat.

Sexy didn't need to respond. She started to dance and wind on the dance floor with the long legged beauty against her. Her hands went from gripping Rochelle's moving hips to holding her close like a child holds a doll. Being up against the long legged Brazilian so close was enticing.

"Damn, I want you," Sexy whispered in the woman's ear.

It caused Rochelle to smile. "You do, huh? How bad?"

"My pussy is dripping wet right now."

"So when and where?"

"The when, right now, and I know someplace where," Sexy replied almost desperately, yearning to taste and fuck her new best friend of the night.

Rochelle's engaging smile was already proof of her answer. Not wasting any more time on the dance floor, Sexy took Rochelle by her hand and led her away from the crowd. She couldn't wait to strip the Brazilian woman stark naked and have her way with her. The heavy thirst was in her eyes, and before they could step foot outside of the club, Sexy was all over Rochelle like tattoos on Lil Wayne.

"I see someone's impatient for it," Rochelle said while chuckling.

I want you bad, baby," Sexy said while planting kisses against her neck and moving her hand in between her thighs.

"Where did you park at?"

"I'm the white Charger at the corner." Sexy wrapped her arm around Rochelle and they proceeded toward the cocaine colored Charger down the street.

Unbeknownst to Sexy, she was being watched keenly. The two ladies laughed and fondled each other publicly under the full moon. When Sexy and Rochelle were near the car, a towering shadow loomed from the darkness and charged at Sexy from behind. He threw her into a tight chokehold and thrust a syringe into her neck. The drug M99, also known as etorphine, quickly took effect, seeping into her bloodstream and causing

Sexy to pass out within seconds. She became listless in her attackers' arms and subsequently thrown into the trunk of her own car.

Rochelle stood impassive by what she saw. Fancy walked toward her and handed her a lumpy envelope containing twenty thousand in cash. The leggy Brazilian smiled widely at such a huge payoff for a few moments of work. She was warned to keep her mouth shut and then strutted back in the direction of the club.

Fancy got behind the wheel of her victim's Dodge Charger and drove away. She had special plans for Sexy—very wicked special plans.

The ice-cold water thrown in Sexy's face abruptly snapped her out of her temporary unconsciousness. She gasped and squirmed from the harsh blast against her. She found herself stripped naked with her arms outstretched and shackled to the ceiling. It took her a short moment to realize her condition and what was going on. She found herself in a barren meat locker with the temperature at 20 degrees and surrounded by Fancy and two unknown men.

She cursed out, "Fuck all y'all!" and then shook rapidly to pull herself free, desperately trying to extricate herself from her restraints, but to no avail. She was in their lair and completely defenseless. The ice water that was thrown on her and the arctic cold of the room made her shiver uncontrollably.

Ozone stepped up with a nozzle to the hose in his hands and let her have it. The cold water splashed against her with tremendous force, almost knocking her back into the wall, but the restraints kept her still. Sexy screamed loudly. The torture went on for several minutes until her teeth chattered and she wanted drop to the ground.

Fancy walked toward her and asked, "Do you know who I am?"

Despite the torture, Sexy still remained defiant. She cursed, "Fuck you!" and spit phlegm into Fancy's face.

Fancy twisted her face in anger and shouted, "Do this bitch again!"

Ozone stepped forward and twisted the nozzle again, causing seventy-five to one hundred PSI of pressure to come pouring out, slamming into Sexy like. She screamed loudly as she was violently tossed around from the serious pressure, but remained dangling because of the restraints around her wrists.

Fancy stood in the background watching stoically. For five minutes, the torture went on. When Ozone was done with the hose, Nasir stepped up and hit Sexy with a few bolts of electricity from sparking jumper cables. The excruciating pain shot through Sexy causing an agonizing scream that seemed to echo endlessly.

Fancy grabbed Sexy by the throat sternly and glared at her. "You tell me what I need to know and I can make this end really fast for you."

Sexy's breathing was sparse from the pain with the bitter cold nipping at her like tiny daggers penetrating her skin. With her fingers pushing into Sexy's neck, Fancy squeezed tightly. Any more pressure and Fancy would be able to see life fade from her eyes. But it was too soon to see her die. The main goal was to extract information from their victim.

"Where's Pippa, and what's her real name?" Fancy demanded.

Sexy refused to answer. She was too stubborn to give up the woman she loved. She shot Fancy a defiant stare and kept silent, which was beginning to infuriate Fancy. She turned to Ozone and said, "Hit her again!"

Ozone stepped up while Fancy took a few steps back. He aimed the nozzle dead at Sexy's naked chest and rotated the nozzle. The cold water came flying out like a bullet. Ozone aimed the nozzle at her face, and the force nearly broke her jaw and almost drowned her. She tried to resist and begged for mercy, but she was finding it hard to scream, let alone speak. When the water stopped running, the jumper cables sparked in Nasir's hands and he connected the fire to her cold, wet nipples . The sound coming from Sexy's mouth sounded inhuman.

It went on for several minutes. When the torturing stopped, Sexy's body looked lifeless as saliva began to drool uncontrollably from her mouth. She was alive, but barely.

Once again, Fancy approached her with a scowl. She stood just inches from Sexy. This time she didn't put any hands on her, but looked at her with contempt.

"Give me her name and the pain stops," Fancy said.

Still silence.

"Hit her again," Fancy behest.

The tormenting act went on several more times, but this time followed by cigarette burns to the face and eye by Fancy. The girl was tough.

"Is it worth it, Sexy? Is it?" Fancy screamed.

Sexy could barely move. She was ready to drop to her knees and die.

"You're a tough fuckin' bitch. I'll give you that," Fancy said to her, showing some admiration for her endurance to pain and love. "But I'm also persistent and this can go on all fuckin' night. I don't care if I have to bring you back from the dead myself, I always get what I want."

Sexy remained silent. It was obvious she was ready to die, but the true torture was that Fancy wouldn't let her. She was going to live until something valuable was said. Fancy eyed her victim. She needed another approach. She needed to get into the bitch's head.

"You know how we found you? Your own sister gave you up."

Sexy slowly lifted her head with one eye bruised, and swollen shut and looked at her incredulously.

"Oh, you think I'm lying. Cindy, right?"

The look on Sexy's face said she believed Fancy.

"Yes. It makes you think, what kind of bitch are you that your own sister is willing to give you up? Crazy," Fancy said. "But if you wanna play these games, then I'll hunt your fuckin' momma down and—"

"You leave my mother out of this!" Sexy screamed out.

"I will if you cooperate with us. Ask yourself if Pippa's life is worth more than your own mommy's? And I promise you that she will get even harsher treatment because you're pissing me the fuck off right now!"

Tears started to trickle from Sexy's eyes. She felt betrayed on so many levels. How could Cindy give her up like that? Was her heart that cold? But she was always a money hungry bitch who only cared about herself. Sexy knew her death was inevitable, but her mom's life had to be spared. It agitated Sexy that Fancy had that leverage on her, because she was ready to die from the torture rather than snitch on the ones she loved.

"You better hurry up and tell me everything you know about this bitch, starting with her real name," Fancy warned.

"Her name is Esmeralda," Sexy uttered faintly.

Fancy smiled. "Esmeralda. What else? Tell me everything or I swear, after your death, I'll cut that bitch into pieces slowly and save her head as my own personal souvenir."

"Her true name is Esmeralda Blanco, and she's the daughter of Griselda Blanco," Sexy said faintly.

"Griselda Blanco's . . . daughter?" Finally, Nasir spoke up.

Reluctantly, Sexy started to talk and everything about Esmeralda came pouring out. Fancy listened intently and so did Nasir and Ozone. It was captivating information for everyone.

Esmeralda was the daughter of the queen of cocaine, La Dama de la Mafia—the black widow, and the Godmother. It was known to them that Griselda was born in Cartagena, Colombia, and when she became a drug lord for the Medellín Cartel, she met Jesus. She had a notorious reputation as did Jesus, and already had three sons from her past marriages when she became pregnant with Jesus' child. While the world thought she had four sons, she really had three. Her fourth child was a girl, Esmeralda, who was shipped off as an infant for protection to live with an aunt. Griselda told everyone, including Jesus, that she had had a boy. And thinking that he had his first son, who was denied to him, Jesus sought revenge. All three of Griselda's sons were murdered, allegedly by Jesus, and several attempts had been made on her life for over three decades. But Griselda had her own power and wasn't easy to assassinate. When Griselda was murdered on September 3rd, Esmeralda sought revenge for her family that had been slaughtered at the hands of her father. She killed his whole family but wanted to get to his prize possession, his son, Pablo.

Jesus wanted a son who would carry his last name and keep his lineage alive long after he was dead. He was a true descendant of Pablo Escobar and named his firstborn son after his idol. Jesus knew that the hit came from Griselda's cartel, but he thought it was from the son he and Griselda created. It was going to be a bombshell to find out that the son he killed for, all the innocent lives that he snuffed out, sacrificing his own daughters, was actually a girl child—a bitter woman who wanted his first and only son dead.

The news was overwhelming for Fancy. It was nothing but civil war—civil rivalry within the Colombian cartel, and somehow she was thrust into the middle of it. But the fact that she had a half-brother and Esmeralda was her half-sister was very disturbing for Fancy. It became mind-boggling. Fancy felt mortified that she'd had sex with the woman who was her sister, even if it was once. Fancy had the urge to throw up and disappear. But her mind was still on revenge. She needed to think.

Fancy looked at Nasir and nodded. Nasir knew what he had to do. He stepped toward Sexy, raised his pistol at her, and Sexy didn't even blink. She yelled, "Do you!"

It was what she wanted, death, so Nasir put a bullet into her head. She slumped with her arms still outstretched, her lifeless body dangling from the ceiling.

CHAPTER 25

Fancy rushed out of the Maybach when it stopped in front of the towering high-rise in downtown Manhattan with fury in her eyes. She felt twisted with emotions, highly upset. The trip to Miami was a success, but she came back knowing the truth about so many things and a lot more baggage about herself. She didn't know what the fuck was going on.

With Sexy dead, she was one up on Esmeralda. It was a satisfactory feeling to not be in the dark any longer. But now things needed to change, and she was going at them full throttle. The crafty bitch came at her hard and she had to let everyone know that she wasn't just pretending to be a gangster—she was one. And the world wasn't going to take advantage of her anymore.

She stormed into the lobby with her heels smashing into the marble pavement, her footsteps echoing as she moved hurriedly toward the elevator. She was going to the penthouse suite on the top floor to see Jesus, or whatever his name was, and demand to see her real father.

Fancy rode the elevator in silence. The only thing on her mind was to expose the impostor and to know who the real Jesus was. It was eating away at her so badly. And then she was itching to find Esmeralda, her half-sister, and have some personal words with her before she blew her damn head off. With Sexy dead, hearing the news of her girlfriend's violent murder,

Esmeralda had to come out of hiding and confront her. They put the word out in Miami about Sexy. They'd disrespected her body, carving "BITCH" in her chest after her death and leaving the body in South Beach with a dildo sticking out her pussy for the public to find.

It became front-page news in Miami.

Fancy entered the penthouse suite, anticipating seeing the imposter again. The place was quiet. She paced around the room. It had been several weeks since they'd spoken. Fancy needed a drink. She was clad in a black pinstripe pantsuit, looking sophisticated and mature. As usual, she walked toward the window and gazed out, her attention fixed on the people below. While thinking about her rise to the top, she heard someone say, "Jesus will meet you in the next room."

Fancy turned around and saw one of their male servants greeting her, unsmiling.

"Where is he?"

"You may follow me. He has been expecting you."

The man pivoted and descended some short stairs into another room. Fancy was right behind him. He escorted her in, and then made his exit, shutting the door behind him. The room was shadowy and decorated in leather furniture arranged oddly, as if someone could hold court there.

The same Jesus was seated on one of the couches, smoking his cigar. He looked calm, lounging with his legs crossed and one arm behind the back of the chair. Fancy glared at him and the first thing out of her mouth to him was, "Sexy's dead! Now I'm looking for Esmeralda! I know she's my sister and wants me dead. I'm going to kill that fuckin' bitch, too! I know everything that y'all tried to hide from me—everything!"

The man stood up, keeping his cool. He took a few pulls from his cigar and remained quiet.

Fancy continued with, "And I know you're not my real fuckin' father! Who are you? And where is he? You used me as bait to catch the killer of your family. I'm his family too, not some fuckin' outcast! I'm his daughter, too! And I'm not that bitch to be played with. I'm not my mother! You hear me! Do you fuckin' hear me!"

He remained stoic. The young girl was becoming out of control, screaming madly. She stormed toward him and once again demanded to know, "Who are you?"

"My name is Carlos, and I'm a close associate of Jesus," he said calmly.

"Where is he?"

Fancy looked around the room and stared at the double-sided mirror. She knew someone was watching her behind it. It didn't take a genius to know it was a two-way mirror. She charged toward it and banged her fist against it and shouted, "Whoever's fuckin' behind this shit, come see me like a man! I'm tired of the fuckin' games with y'all! I wanna know who you are. Who's the real Jesus? Come out of there, Jesus, and meet your daughter!"

"You're wasting your time, Fancy," said Carlos.

"And why you think that?"

Unbeknownst to Fancy, the room on the other side of the mirror was only filled with several of the cartel's henchman. There was a camera aimed at the furnished room from behind the mirror, and Jesus wasn't anywhere around. Her father was actually in Paris, France with his son, Pablo, and his new wife, living a peaceful life. He observed the entire scene unfolding with Fancy and Carlos via satellite.

Jesus sat in his lavishly decorated Paris office with a stunning view of the Eiffel Tower outside his window. He was seated behind his large desk with the thirty-inch flat-screen clearly showing the events transpiring over four thousand miles away. He composedly watched his daughter lose control in his New York penthouse. She was like wildfire. If he could have felt some sort of remorse for using his own daughter as a sheep to catch the wolves, he didn't. He didn't even feel any guilt for having Fancy think that one of his trusted lieutenants, who wasn't even related to him, was her father.

Jesus was an aging man, but a very dangerous man still. He wasn't moved by anything. But he was very grateful that she completed a task that she didn't even know was handed to her—which was finding the person or persons who were threatening his family—his beloved family. And for that, Jesus felt loyal to her, and unbeknownst to Fancy, he would watch over her for the rest of his life. No harm would ever come to Fancy as long as he could help it.

Jesus was a heartless man with so much power that he almost seemed like a mystical crime figure—and to the majority, he was a god. He was the boogieman in the underworld. He had power, and his power was able to get results.

He owned the building in Paris; he owned many buildings in several countries, including the one in Manhattan. He owned the world. He hadn't been in the States for several years and always lived or traveled aboard. But he always monitored everything going on, from his multibillion-dollar empire to his family. And now he was monitoring Fancy go crazy like she had lost her mind.

Jesus stared at the computer monitor stoically and smoked his high-priced Cuban cigar. He fixed his concentration on her because she was such a class act, watching the entertainment in privacy.

Fancy repeatedly banged her fists against the double sided mirror, attempting to break it. "I want to meet you! Come out and fuckin' meet me, Jesus! Right now! No more fuckin' games with you! Why can't you come out and meet your own damn daughter?"

The tears started to stream from her eyes. She was seething with rage and didn't care anymore.

"I fuckin' survived! I'm a survivor, Father, and you need to know that. You can't use me anymore. I'm building my own empire, one more powerful than yours," she screamed.

Her emotions were strong and her tears so heavy, they began to leave a puddle on the floor.

"Stop it," Carlos whispered. "Act like a lady."

"Why?"

"You're just wasting your time. Jesus is a man that never wants to be seen."

Fancy dried her tears and turned to look at Carlos. She finally figured it out. "He's not even here, is he?"

Carlos stood silently.

Fancy fell to her knees in defeat. She breathed heavily and felt like her heart would stop. Carlos came close and stood over her. She looked up at him and locked eyes.

"Where is he?" she asked dejectedly.

Carlos stared at her coldly. He too was unmoved by her tears and emotions.

"You will be well taken care of," he replied nonchalantly. "You have been very helpful to our organization."

Fancy didn't care for anything he had to say. "Fuck you, Hunky!"

Nasir had just stepped out of the shower when he heard his cell phone ringing in the next room. He hurried to answer it. It was Pete from the block calling him. Answering the phone, he knew it had to be important for Pete to call him in the morning. With Fancy away on business and him fresh back from Miami, he was itching to get back to business. It felt good to be back in New York.

"Pete, talk to me," Nasir said, toweling off in the bedroom.

"I got some news for you, Nasir," Pete said.

"Then talk to me."

"We found him," said Pete.

"Found who? Pete, stop fuckin' double talkin' me and say who?"

"Li'l-Un."

Hearing that name made Nasir ready to run out the house in his towel and jump into his Benz almost naked to go see that muthafucka.

"I'll be in Brooklyn within a heartbeat," he hollered.

Nasir hurriedly got dressed and rushed outside, jumping into his Benz. He drove toward Brooklyn like he was in a drag race. It had been too long since Li'l-Un first went on the run from him. Nasir always held grudges, but this time it was personal between the two of them. Nasir felt responsible for his little brother's murder because the streets exposed that it was Li'l-Un who had murdered Al-Saadiq during the attempt on his life after Lisa's birthday party. Li'l-Un was trying to take over the streets. He had put together his own violent crew and was ready to war with Nasir. If Nasir had killed Li'l-Un while he had the chance in his mother's apartment, then his little brother would still have been alive.

It took him forty minutes to arrive in Brooklyn, where he was greeted by Pete, Dibbs, and a few other goons on the block. Nasir jumped out of his ride and headed toward them with his lips twisted in disgust. He had a .45 tucked snugly in his waistband and was bloodthirsty for revenge. The death of Al-Saadiq wasn't going unsolved. He quickly held court on the block with his young goons closely listening. The only thing Nasir wanted to know was where Lil-Un was. And thanks to a crackhead snitch, he knew of his whereabouts.

"He in an apartment in the Van Dyke Houses on the low, and the nigga came back heavily armed, Nasir, they sayin' he ready to war wit' you," said Dibbs.

Nasir didn't care about him being heavily armed. If Li'l-Un wanted a war, then he was about to get one really soon. Nasir only wanted revenge, and he was going to get it. Looking aloof from the news he'd just received, he climbed back into his Benz with Dibbs riding shotgun and headed toward the Van Dyke housing project. Tonight, his beef with Li'l-Un would end one way or the other.

Two cars full of goons pulled up to the housing project and multiple doors flew open with numerous goons jumping out. Nasir led the charge into the project building flanked by Pete, Dibbs, and two other men. They ascended the concrete stairway toward the sixth floor and gripped their guns. Coming to the door of their target, Nasir looked at Dibbs and asked, "You sure this is the right apartment?"

He nodded.

Rap music could be heard blaring inside. Nasir was ready to kick in the door, burst in and shoot everything moving. With four men at the door, and only one way in or out of the apartment, Li'l-Un was trapped like a rat.

Thinking about his little brother and seething with rage, Nasir couldn't wait any longer. He lifted his foot and decided to kick in the door and go in blazing—fuck it! He was a beast and there was no rational thinking when it came to anyone fucking with his family.

Having the element of surprise, the men went in shooting first, with the occupants of the apartment caught off guard not knowing if it was police or stickup kids. They quickly reacted to the explosion coming through the front door, but were a little too late. Gunfire was heard over the loud rap music. Two men seated on the couch by the door caught four bullets to their chests, and another stranger caught a slug to his head by the kitchen entrance. Nasir moved through the apartment like lightening while Dibbs and Pete took care of their foes in the living room.

Nasir kicked in the bedroom door and damn near got his head blown off by a shotgun blast that tore through the doorframe behind him.

"Yeah, what now, bitch? Fuck you, nigga! Fuck you! You should have killed me when you had the chance!" Li'l-Un screamed.

Nasir was ready to take his advice.

The naked young girl Li'l-Un was in bed with screamed louder. Li'l-Un leaped from the bed with the shotgun in his hand and continued to fire at Nasir. Nasir hit the floor and retreated back into the hallway. Li'l-Un knew it was a wrap. He tried to escape out the window, and being six floors up, it was an incredible act. Perched on the windowsill with one foot dangling out the window and the other in the bedroom, he was ready to make the jump and take his chances with the fall rather than face Nasir.

Nasir charged back into the bedroom and fired rapidly at Li'l-Un. Two shots tore into Li'l-Un's thin frame and he went flying out the window.

Nasir ran over to witness his death, but surprisingly, Li'l-Un survived the fall and being shot twice after landing on a heap of trash. He managed to pick himself up and limp toward the courtyard, but he was hurt badly.

"Muthafucka!" Nasir shouted.

He thrust the gun out the window and aimed at a crippled Li'l-Un trying to escape the danger. Nasir squeezed, and the tip of his .45 lit up like a Roman candle.

Bak! Bak! Bak! Bak!

When the gunfire stopped, Li'l-Un's body lay still on the ground. Nasir gazed at the body for a moment. He breathed heavily. It was a bittersweet victory. What was done tonight should have been done at his mother's apartment, but he hadn't wanted to kill anyone in front of Brenda.

"Ohmygod! Ohmygod!" the naked woman screamed frantically.

Nasir glared at her. The coldness in his eyes intimated his next action. Suddenly, he lifted his gun and fired two shots into the screaming woman, leaving her slumped against the bed frame. He couldn't leave behind any witnesses. He and his cronies made their speedy exit from the apartment and the building, hearing police sirens blaring in the background.

Nasir jumped behind the wheel of his Benz, looking somewhat detached from the scenario and the earsplitting, blue-and-red-lit trouble coming their way. He hesitated in driving away from the crime scene, which started to worry Pete and Dibbs.

"Nasir, c'mon! Let's go, man. Let's get the fuck outta here!" Pete hollered.

Nasir sat there, looking like a zombie.

"Nasir, c'mon…let's go!" Pete and Dibbs screamed collectively.

Still, he didn't respond.

"Fuck this, we out!" Pete shouted.

They swung open the doors and sprang from the car and became track stars on the streets, leaving Nasir behind. He'd lost his mind—snapped. It seemed like he wanted to get caught. Nasir continued to sit still with the murder weapon in his hand. The blue and red lights were approaching fast and within minutes, they emerged onto the block like a swarm of bees with their guns drawn and aimed at Nasir.

"Driver, get out the car now!" the police warned.

Nasir remained still. He remained seated in his car and acted like they weren't there at all.

"Driver, put your hands out the window and slowly remove yourself from the vehicle and lie face-down on the concrete. Now!"

Nasir gripped the pistol in his hand and looked around. He was surrounded by police lights shining heavily in his car. Instead of going out like a warrior, in a hail of bullets, he did what he was told and slowly removed himself from the car and went to lay facedown against the concrete. He was surrendering himself, but to who or what, Nasir didn't have any clue. He was just tired of it all. Police swarmed on top of him madly and bent his arms around his back, and placed the handcuffs on him.

Nasir remained cool. He knew his arrest was going to upset Fancy. He closed his eyes as he was led away by police and thrown into the back of a marked police car.

This was it, a new chapter in his life.

EPILOGUE

It would be Jesus' gift to Fancy. Esmeralda—her location, along with all of her crew, snuffed out. Jesus had arranged for everyone connected to Esmeralda to be brutally murdered—they could run, but they couldn't hide from the billionaire crime lord. And the first to be murdered was Rise. They found his headless body in the trunk of a parked Lexus around the corner from Miami's City Hall with his head placed strategically on the dashboard. It was a bold statement sent by the cartel.

Another victim connected to Esmeralda was found murdered in his bathtub. He was shot in both eyes and in the neck, the water he was soaking in turned crimson from the blood oozing from the body. The third victim was thrown into a lion's pit at the zoo, and he was immediately torn apart by the hungry animals. When the zookeepers and detectives found him, there wasn't much left of him but remnants of what used to be a full-grown man. And the fifth victim was found burned to death in the front seat of a charred SUV. His throat was cut from ear to ear and the charred body was unrecognizable—it was going to take dental records to identify the body.

Esmeralda was the last one standing. They said she had left the country, flown off to some remote location in the West Indies, or maybe Colombia, and was in hiding from the cartel. She had gone off the radar, closed down her beauty salon, sold her homes and apartment, and didn't want to be seen anywhere in the country.

But Fancy wasn't going to give up finding her. With Nasir incarcerated, she had to rebuild her shooters, and her empire wasn't going to stop thriving. Fancy wanted to become a legend. But with her half-sister Esmeralda still lurking out there, Fancy felt she would never have peace until the bitch was dead. Even when the truth behind Al-Saadiq's death came to light, Fancy felt Esmeralda was still responsible somehow.

An anonymous phone call to Fancy suddenly revealed Esmeralda's location. She was hiding out in a beach house in Bahamas. It was the news she had been waiting for. Fancy took a private jet to the Bahamas and arrived early Sunday morning in the tropical paradise.

She took a private car service from the airport to the beach house. The area was vast, and with the tropical breeze and blankets of soft sand and blue water, its serenity belied the terror that was about to happen. Fancy slowly made her way toward the beach home that looked like diamonds on the sand. It was a beautiful place, secluded from the public, and also a quiet getaway location that was supposed to be on the low. But today, it would be a place where someone's life—either Fancy's or Esmeralda's—was going to end.

Fancy was armed with a .9mm. She crept inside the home. It was still and decorated tastefully with light from the fading sun percolating through the floor-to-ceiling windows. When Fancy entered the living room, she came face-to-face with Esmeralda, who was clad in a T-shirt and sweats. They glared at each other. Esmeralda shot her look down to the gun in Fancy's hand. Fancy had the advantage. Both ladies remained quiet with their intense glares speaking more loudly.

It could have easily been a homicide; Fancy could shoot and kill, but this beef between them had become a lot more personal. They both had too much to prove. "You have a lot of murders you need to answer for,"

Fancy said through clenched teeth.

Esmeralda smirked. She wasn't intimidated by Fancy and the gun. She boldly replied, "Fuck you, bitch!"

"Not today, bitch! Not ever again." Fancy shouted.

Esmeralda wasn't expecting Jesus to send Fancy after her. She assumed it would be one of his highly skilled contract killers. What game was he playing? Why send Fancy?

"So he sends you to do the dirty work," Esmeralda said mockingly with a sinister grin spread across her face. "Put the fuckin' gun down and come make me pay. Or are you just here to talk?"

"I see you find this shit amusing."

Esmeralda shot back. "I find you very amusing."

Esmeralda went over to the glass coffee table and reached for her cigarettes. Fancy outstretched her arm and aimed the pistol at her head. She sternly warned, "Move again, bitch, and I'll put two in your fuckin' head!"

"A little jumpy, eh?" Esmeralda let out a hysterical laugh. "Relax. I was only reaching for my Newports. If you wanted to shoot me in the back, you had the drop on me when you first came through them doors. I'm guessing you have something else in mind."

Both women's eyes bore holes into each other. The hate between them wasn't lost. Fancy regretted the day she brought Esmeralda into her life.

"The only thing in my mind is seeing you leave here in a body bag."

Esmeralda chuckled. "That shit ain't happening."

Fancy was incredulous. She was standing with a gun in her hand, and Esmeralda was still taking shit? Unbelievable.

"You sound stupid."

"I sound confident. Put the gun down and show me what you're made of. Unless you're scared . . ."

"No shook hands in Brook-land, bitch!" Fancy stated.

"You're a fuckin' punk. I can see fear all in your eyes."

"Never that."

Esmeralda smiled. "How do you want to do this?" She cracked her knuckles and was ready to go blow for blow with Fancy.

Fancy placed the gun in the chair next to her and responded, "I see you wanna toss it up, fight to the death in this fancy place of yours."

Fancy stepped out of her stilettos one by one, getting ready for battle.

Esmeralda's smile told her that she liked the idea. "That's exactly what I wanna do. But I must warn you, the odds aren't in your favor."

Outside of the beach house, the ocean waves were heard crashing against the shoreline, and there weren't any people around to enjoy the scenery. It was a secluded beach and residents in the area paid handsomely for their privacy. The isolation was going to work for one of the ladies and against the other.

Esmeralda took a hearty pull on her cigarette, enjoying the nicotine, and then extinguished it in an ashtray nearby. Unbeknownst to Fancy, Esmeralda had trained in kickboxing and considered herself lethal without a gun. She didn't need a weapon to handle Fancy.

Esmeralda charged at her sister, screaming with rage with her fists clamped together. She was ready to do some bodily harm. Fancy reached for her second pistol, the .380 she kept hidden on her thigh, and put a bullet directly in Esmeralda's forehead. The look of shock plastered on her face said it all. Esmeralda's body didn't drop immediately. She took a couple steps backward, almost as if she were trying to get her bearings, and then collapsed.

Fancy stood over her dead body and screamed, "What do you see in my eyes now? Huh? You still see fear? You wanna know what I see? I see dead!"

Fancy screamed at the corpse like a crazy woman until she couldn't scream anymore. Her voice became hoarse and she felt weary. She had been through too much. There wasn't any way Fancy was going one-on-one with Esmeralda. Her mother didn't raise a fool.

The front door of the beach house opened, and only one survivor stepped out. Mentally, Fancy was exhausted. But she was alive.

Fancy slowly made her way toward the beach with the gun gripped loosely in her hand. She was in tears. She fell to her knees against the sand and gazed out into the ocean. It was a beautiful scene as the waves crashed the shoreline. Fancy had thought that killing Esmeralda would give her some relief, but it didn't. She felt it was only the beginning. There was a time in her life when she'd thought she was an only child; now she'd just murdered one sister and found out that she had a brother and her other two sisters were killed in Colombia.

She tossed the gun into the ocean and sat in the sand for a long time, contemplating her next move. She had crossed an enemy off the list, but her payback wasn't done.

Now, all she had to do was find Pablo.

That little muthafucka was going to pay for her pain.